The Final Campaign
of the American Revolution

Illustration 1. Frigate *South Carolina* by John Phippen, 1793. Courtesy of the Peabody Museum of Salem, Mass. Photo by Mark Sexton.

JAMES A. LEWIS

THE FINAL CAMPAIGN OF THE AMERICAN REVOLUTION

Rise and Fall of the Spanish Bahamas

University of South Carolina Press

The Spanish Embassy awarded *The Final Campaign of the American Revolution: Rise and Fall of the Spanish Bahamas* second prize in its juried contest: "Spain and America in the Quincentennial of the Discovery."

Copyright © University of South Carolina, 1991
Published in Columbia, South Carolina, by the
University of South Carolina Press

Manufactured in the United States of America

Library of Congress Cataloging-in-Publication Data

Lewis, James A., 1942–
    The final campaign of the American Revolution: rise and fall of
the Spanish Bahamas / James A. Lewis.
        p.   cm.
    Includes bibliographical references and index.
    ISBN 0-87249-726-7 (alk. paper)
    1. West Indies—History—1775–1783.   2. Bahamas—History.
3. Spaniards—Bahamas—History—18th century.   I. Title.
E263.W5L46   1991
972.9'03—dc20   90–48933

For
Alice Lewis

CONTENTS

MAPS AND ILLUSTRATIONS

PREFACE

The topic of this book is one of those subjects that historians stumble across pursuing other matters. While working on my dissertation—a study of Mexico during the American Revolution—now ever so many years ago, I was struck by how important the Spanish Caribbean, particularly Cuba, was to the affairs of that period. Once done with my dissertation, I turned my attention to the Cuba of the 1770s and 1780s, where I kept encountering information on the Spanish expedition against the Bahamas in 1782 and the numerous problems associated with ruling that captured territory. I decided to make this subject a chapter in a large book on the entire Spanish empire during the American Revolution, but my topic simply grew from chapter length to one meriting (I think) a book of its own.

The Final Campaign explores a number of historical problems. It shows, despite much Bicentennial and Columbus hoopla, just how tenuous and fragile the cooperation between Bourbon Spain and republican United States was against their common foe—Great Britain. Old fears, hatreds, and prejudices going far back into the historical past of both peoples did not disappear overnight during the American Revolution.

This work also examines the important and neglected field of Spanish bureaucracy during wartime. Reformed, streamlined, and energized by political changes brought about by competent monarchs and ministers in Madrid, Spanish bureaucrats still suffered from internal rifts which hindered their ability to move in a united, efficient manner. The two branches of the Spanish military—its army and navy—did not get along, and each spent long hours laying brilliant campaigns to scuttle the successes of the other. Spanish treasury and administrative officials resented each other's pretensions so much that the two flooded the mails back to Spain with complaints, rumors, and charges of corruption and incompetence against the other.

Residents of the Bahamas also receive due attention in this study. They too were divided, divided enough to put up no resistance against the invaders in 1782, divided enough that some became active collaborators with the foreign conquerors. Although the colony was a loyalist bastion after 1783, crown officials in London had good reason to suspect the fidelity of this lonely Caribbean outpost throughout the war. The immediate aftermath of the war in the Bahamas was a significant period in the history of the colony, and the manner in which New Providence became British again had important ramifications for future events in that colony and elsewhere.

I owe a number of debts in completing the work, the interest and capital of which I can only pay back with words. My own institution, Western Carolina University, has been most generous with its very limited funds for research. Only those academicians who labor in the vineyards of regional schools with heavy teaching loads and very modest research funds will know how important a few hundred dollars here and there can be. I have also received help from the American Philosophical Society to microfilm materials in England. The National Endowment for the Humanities paid for one of my research trips. What did scholars do before the NEH existed? The University of Florida generously awarded me a grant to use its rich Latin American collection. The Spanish Ministry of Culture kindly judged a manuscript version of this work worthy of one of its "Spain and America in the Quincentennial of the Discovery" prizes for 1988.

Numerous individuals have taken time from their busy schedules to aid me in countless ways. Carole Troxler, Wylma Wates, Francisco Sánchez Rico, Light Cummins, J. Leitch Wright, Jr., William Anderson, Lewis Sutton, Cary Graham, Tony Hickey, Gary White, and D. Gail Saunders have generously lent me their expertise. Max R. Williams and Johanna O. Lewis have read and reread my manuscript. They now know more about *The Final Campaign* than any person really should. Joe Ginn, Regina Hall, and Deborah Edwards have graciously typed and retyped this manuscript. My family has stood by me and wondered whether I would ever finish. I too have pondered the same question. Lastly, I would like to thank my father, a man who consciously or not taught me something about the value of work, and John Tate Lanning, a mentor who taught me something about scholarship. I only wish that I had thought to thank both of them while they still lived.

Chapter One

GATHERING STORM

The Bahamas, more commonly called in the eighteenth century New Providence, were a British possession almost as radically affected by the American Revolution as were the Thirteen Colonies. Geography alone decreed that this Caribbean outpost would be battered by the powerful waves of change churned up during the war years. Perched at the northernmost point of the Caribbean, New Providence was the closest island possession of Great Britain to the rebellion on the mainland. Only the Two Floridas and Canada, both with land borders, lay closer to these continental upheavals. Events in Philadelphia, New York, or Charleston often had immediate implications for Nassau, capital of the Bahamas. While linkage north was important in determining the colony's involvement in the war, so too were the ocean's currents and winds to the south and west. Almost the entire export commerce of the western Caribbean, New Spain, Louisiana, Central America, and the ports of Cartagena and Panama passed New Providence, which was situated alongside two major exits from the Gulf of Mexico, the Old and New Bahama Channels. In the eighteenth century, war typically followed the routes of commerce. Fated to be so close to much of the action of the war, they were often part of action. Occupied four times in eight years of war by invading forces, the Bahamas fell to new masters often. The most significant of these temporary masters was Spain, which invaded, occupied, and lost the colony during the last year of the war from 1782 to 1783.

1

Despite being relegated by many American historians to the position of a minor participant in the war, Spain was a major military factor in the conflict as early as 1775. The possibility of Spanish intervention in the war, along with that of their Bourbon cousins in France, caused Great Britain to retain in Europe a large part of its military might. After having declared war against Britain in 1779, Spain directed the largest and longest campaign of the war, the siege of Gibraltar, from 1779 to 1783. At its peak this operation tied down over 30,000 regulars on both sides, in addition to the naval forces involved, dwarfing all campaigns in the western hemisphere.[1] It was Spain that handed England its greatest setback in Europe, the loss of Minorca in 1782. With the exception of affairs on the continent of North America, it was also Spanish ambition in the Caribbean which most concerned the British in the New World.

That Spain should play a major role in the war from 1775 to 1783 was understandable. Under the tutelage of the Bourbons in the eighteenth century, particularly during the reign of Charles III (1759–88), Spain reemerged as a substantial and confident European power. Spanish vigor was especially evident in its revitalized empire and the appearance of an impressive navy, third in size only to England and France by the 1770s. While Hapsburg Spain in the sixteenth and seventeenth centuries confronted an entire Europe that was hostile, Bourbon Spain concerned itself primarily with the British. Only Great Britain had the potential and the interest to damage Spain's empire. Affairs in London, hence, were of vital concern to Madrid.

When trouble erupted in the British colonies in 1775, the government of Charles III reacted to the revolt cautiously and conservatively.[2] Spanish interest in the affairs of English America was partly curiosity. Europe was not accustomed to colonial disturbances of this nature. Yet the Spanish government also detected something that was apparent to other rivals of Great Britain: this colonial conflict provided Spain with an opportunity to settle old scores and recover lost territory. England's powerful navy had time and again frustrated continental coalitions against Great Britain in the eighteenth century, but never before had circumstances forced the British to divert part of their military strength to retain the allegiance of their own possessions. France, even more eager than Spain to see a humbled England, took advantage of its old adversary's colonial distractions to declare war in 1778. Spain would follow suit.

Yet Spain's declaration of war did not come until June 1779, over a year after the French. In Spain's previous conflict with England, that from 1762 to 1763 during the waning days of the Seven Years' War, the government of Charles III had badly mistimed its entry into the fray and found itself facing England almost alone outside Europe. Spain lost both Havana and Manila within a span of a few months. These painful memories dictated a cautious approach to Britain's new difficulties, but they were not the only reason for a delayed Spanish response to the war. Unlike the French, the Spaniards had no romantic or any other attachment to the cause of the rebellious Anglo-Americans. Those few who understood the significance of the revolt in the New World did not approve. Spain, after all, was a colonial power in its own right, and republicanism held little attraction for informed Spaniards who had seen the results of enlightened monarchial rule under the Bourbons. A rush to help the American rebels held no appeal for the Spanish government. Spain acted to help itself in 1779, and then only when it became obvious that too much caution might result in a lost opportunity to weaken England.

Besides the general objective of revenge against England, Spain had two specific military objectives. In Europe the government wanted desperately to recover Gibraltar, a strategic outpost lost to the British during the War of Spanish Succession earlier in the century. Gibraltar was to Spain what Calais had been to the French for so long, an enclave intolerable in the hands of another country for reasons of national pride. In the New World the ultimate prize was Jamaica, like Gibraltar lost to the British in weaker times. While Spain failed to recover either of these former possessions during the four years of war from 1779 to 1783, Charles III still succeeded in humbling his enemy because his government was willing to entertain other projects in pursuit of the right moment to press a final assault on Gibraltar or Jamaica. New Providence was one of these secondary objectives.

José de Gálvez, minister of the Indies, was the architect of Spanish war plans for the New World.[3] Gálvez took over this key post in 1776, one of many bureaucrats in Bourbon Spain who rose to positions of power principally on merit and ability. Gálvez focused Spanish attention on reconquering Jamaica, well aware from his position in the government of the wealth lost to the British through this colony. He also entertained other objectives for royal forces in the New World. Indeed, he expected more that just the recapture of Jamaica. Gálvez felt that East and West Florida could now be retaken since both were isolated from other English possessions. The Mosquito Coast under British control had long been a nuisance to the Kingdom of Guatemala, and the Spanish minister slated this Central American strip of land for reconquest. He also added New Providence to the list of Spanish targets. In the hands of Spain, to whom these islands had belonged in the days of Columbus, the Bahamas would assure Madrid a safer and more secure Caribbean for imperial commerce.

As a veteran of many years of public service Gálvez understood that military success in the New World depended upon many things. Yet having a group of officials in place who could work together was crucial. New World campaigns required the cooperation of numerous individuals and many different agencies, some semiautonomous and all jealous of their own jurisdictions. As minister of the Indies Gálvez exercised vast powers of patronage, powers that he manipulated skillfully before and after 1779 to make certain that the right individuals were in place in the Caribbean. Although Gálvez did not have authority over the Spanish army or navy, he did have freedom to select military officers for civilian posts. Civilian and military careers in the Spanish bureaucracy of the eighteenth century were interchangeable. By placing highly ranked officers in the proper Indies posts, Gálvez could assume that these men would take control of military operations in their areas.

By 1781 Gálvez had his team of officials, his *equipo*, in place. The principal figure was General Bernardo de Gálvez, his nephew. Young Gálvez, then thirty-five years old, was commander of the Spanish expeditionary army stationed in Havana. This was the force that would undertake any offensive against the British. Bernardo's meteoric rise in rank stemmed from an earlier appointment by his uncle to the governorship of Louisiana, a post that Bernardo used at the beginning of the war to strike against the British in the Mississippi River Valley. Bernardo's immediate second, at least initially, was General Juan Manuel de Cagigal. Cagigal came to the Indies in 1780 as one of the officers sent from Cádiz with reinforcements for Havana. He was an experienced Indies hand, having lived in Cuba as a youngster when his father governed the city of Santiago. The minister of the Indies moved quickly to make Cagigal governor and captain general of Havana, charged with the critical task of defending that key Spanish fortress. Charles III and his ministers wanted no repetition of the military disasters of the previous war. One of the most interesting figures of the Gálvez *equipo* was Francisco de Saavedra, a young bureaucrat from the ministry of the Indies whose assignment was to serve as a roving troubleshooter. Saavedra had instructions to secure the cooperation of overlapping military and administrative units in the area, work with allies (particularly the French at Cape François in modern Haiti), and to encourage maximum contributions of men, supplies, and money from the viceroyalty of New Spain as well as from other less threatened areas of the empire.

Admiral José de Solano was the last major figure in the Spanish *equipo*. Solano commanded the Spanish navy stationed at Havana, supervising the most powerful fleet on permanent station in the Caribbean. He was politically powerful and possessed the temperament to use his ships aggressively. The admiral was the one figure in this Spanish foursome whose position did not depend on the patronage of Gálvez. Yet there had been an earlier connection between Solano and the minister. Solano had served as governor of Santo Domingo from 1771 to 1778. Although these four men did not necessarily like each other, in combination they were formidable.[4] But Spanish plans in the New World were so ambitious that there were bound to be unexpected problems and delays. These hitches had much to do with shaping the New Providence expedition.

The first difficulty that all New World projects faced was the allocation of resources. As crucial as the American empire was to the Spanish government, it was thousands of miles away from Europe. Gibraltar was much closer to home. The campaign against this British outpost had first claim on all military resources, particularly during the initial months of the war when hope ran high in Madrid that this gateway to the Mediterranean would be recovered quickly. The Caribbean was by no means starved for resources, but the military buildup in Havana was slow, particularly in the number of full regiments which could be allocated for expeditions. At the same time internal disorders and uncertainties in three of the four American viceroyalties (Túpac Amaru in Peru, 1780–82; the Comuñeros disturbances in New Granada, 1781–82; and the Izúcar de Matamoros disorders in New Spain, 1781) made other New World officials reluctant to shift military units on the continent to Havana in spite of orders to do so.[5] Thus the concentration of Spanish military forces proceeded at a lethargic pace.

Meanwhile Spanish plans in America suffered from the misfortunes of weather. Crown officials had prudently made certain that some forces needed to attack the British were already in Cuba before the war started. Because Bernardo de Gálvez was governor of Louisiana in 1779, British West Florida became one of the first targets for the aggressive Spaniards. Although Gálvez was able to clear the Mississippi River of British forces and to take Mobile in 1780, Pensacola, the British capital of the colony, had a sizable garrison and could be taken only by launching an attack from Havana, where sufficient men, ships, and supplies lay waiting. Rushing to keep Spanish momentum going and the British on the defensive, Gálvez decided to risk an expedition against Pensacola during hurricane season. His luck failed him. On 17 October 1780 an extremely strong storm caught his fleet barely out of Havana and scattered the helpless ships throughout the Gulf of Mexico and the Caribbean. Gálvez survived to lead a second attack on Pensacola four months later.[6] Nevertheless, the capture of West Florida's capital was delayed long enough to affect the timetable for operations against Jamaica and other British colonies such as New Providence.

Even the French conspired to reduce the speed of the Spanish activities in the Caribbean. As eager as the Castilians were to deal the English a stunning blow, the conquest of Jamaica required help from the French, especially the assistance of a substantial French fleet. With little empire to protect during the 1770s, the French navy was unusually free by eighteenth-century standards to operate against its enemies anywhere in the world. The Spanish navy did not have this measure of freedom. Not until the summer of 1781, however, did the French assign an armada to the Caribbean which could be used to shield the Spanish campaign against Jamaica. Admiral de Grasse commanded this squadron. Because the British in Pensacola resisted until the early summer of 1781, there was not enough time that year for the Spaniards to reconcentrate their forces in Havana, arrange a rendezvous with the admiral, plan the attack on Jamaica, and miss the hurricane season beginning in August. As a result Gálvez, Saavedra, Cagigal, and Solano thought it wise to release de Grasse to function elsewhere. Freed from his principal obligation of helping the Spaniards in 1781, the French admiral sailed north, ultimately contacting the forces of Washington at Yorktown.

Before de Grasse left for the Chesapeake Bay, he met with Saavedra at Cape François and worked out the details for a 1782 spring expedition against Jamaica.[7] It was absolutely vital that the Spanish forces be ready to board ship when the admiral returned south. The Cape François agreement provided that the spring rendezvous would take place in St. Domingue, requiring the Spanish army to relocate from Havana to the French colony. Concentrating forces in St. Domingue had the advantage of allowing the admiral to return to a French port in the Caribbean, pick up a prepared Spanish army and any available French troops, and be in a position for a rapid move toward the Jamaican coast. Since the Spanish navy would transport Bernardo de Gálvez and the expeditionary army to the Cape, this plan required that Solano's forces cover St. Domingue as well as Cuba. By the fall of 1781 the Spanish *equipo* in Havana was making every effort to transport the necessary Spanish regiments to the Cape. Projects such as the invasion of New Providence almost disappeared in the flurry of activities surrounding the Jamaican preparations. Yet the New Providence campaign was still possible if circumstances were fortuitous and if it did not hinder more important preparations.

Before the rush to move to Cape François, Bernardo de Gálvez had expected to conduct the New Providence campaign himself. Military victories in the New World, even modest ones, translated into political capital for himself and his family back in Spain. Indeed, while de Grasse's fleet was at Yorktown, Gálvez had prepared a small force to sail against Nassau in the fall of 1781. Unfavorable weather, something Gálvez did not wish to experience twice, forced cancellation of this initial attempt.[8] Convinced that an attack on the Bahamas would be a short venture, Gálvez still wanted to see it happen. But the increasing demands on the Spanish general as commander in chief forced him to delegate the New Providence project to others. There were several likely subordinates suitable for the post, notably Colonel Luis Huet, a Spanish officer and engineer who had spent considerable time planning the Bahamian strike for Gálvez. He clearly expected the command.[9] Gálvez, however, chose Juan Manuel de Cagigal, member of the *equipo* and captain general of Havana.

Even though Cagigal had been assigned an extremely important task in the Jamaican preparations, that of protecting Havana and keeping Gálvez supplied in St. Domingue, several military and political reasons led Gálvez to turn over the New Providence project to Cagigal. The captain general was an able military officer who had played a dynamic role in the Spanish success at Pensacola by bringing reinforcements at just the right time. Cagigal's family was distinguished, having produced some five lieutenant generals in the eighteenth century alone.[10] Most crucial, however, was the fact that this particular Cagigal had benefited from the patronage powers of José de Gálvez. He could be trusted to do his job and not undercut Bernardo de Gálvez, who was preparing for a more important event at the Cape. These Gálvez-Cagigal ties would soon deteriorate, but they were extremely strong during the final preparations for Jamaica.

Cagigal officially received his appointment to lead the expedition against the Bahamas on 20 January 1782.[11] This was the same month that Gálvez departed for the Cape, soon to be followed by much of the Spanish army in Havana. Gálvez left behind in Cuba some regular troops, who were to form the core of Cagigal's small expeditionary force. The captain general supplemented his small army with contingents drawn from the permanent garrison at Havana. With the memory of 1762 fresh in most minds, stripping any strength from the Havana garrison was risky. Yet the passive conduct of British forces in the Caribbean up to this point made use of Havana troops less a gamble than it might have been during earlier conflicts. Gálvez expected Cagigal to execute his task quickly because both the captain general and his unattached regiments would be needed by Gálvez at the Cape in time to meet de Grasse. It was Cagigal's responsibility to arrange an escort and transportation of the Spanish army from Havana to New Providence and then on to the Cape. Neither Gálvez nor Cagigal, however, expected much help from Solano and the Spanish navy.

Although José de Solano was indeed part of the Spanish *equipo* at Havana, he was the one member over whom José de Gálvez exercised the least leverage. This was unfortunate because a bitter rivalry existed between the Spanish army and navy during the 1770s and 1780s. The minister of the Indies had hoped that his hand-picked team would somehow bridge this dangerous rift. That it could not was due primarily to a series of events during the war which intensified hard feelings between the services. In 1775 the crown had sponsored a major campaign in North Africa against Algiers. This effort ended disastrously, in part because the two services preferred defeat at the hands of a common foe over cooperation. Once war with England came in 1779, moreover, it was the army's view that the Spanish navy had performed very poorly at the siege of Gibraltar. This fratricide within the military easily crossed the Atlantic. The navy supervised all convoys bringing reinforcements to the New World. Most important of these convoys had been that of 1780, which brought many of the regiments that would eventually be mobilized by Gálvez for his Jamaican expedition. Because the navy had loaded most of the regiments many weeks before finally sailing, the voyage of this convoy had caused terrible suffering from disease among the soldiers. To the army the Spanish navy had been insensitive to the effects of a dilatory ocean-crossing on troops.

Most immediate and divisive of all issues between the branches had been an unexpected and embarrassing disagreement at Pensacola in 1781. Final stages of this siege required that the king's ships cross under fire a dangerous sandbar at the entrance to the port. Unless the navy took this course and found a safe anchorage in the harbor, adverse weather would eventually force it to leave for the open sea, making it difficult for land forces to deny supplies and relief to the garrison. Naval commanders had at first refused to risk their ships by running the bar in order to make operations ashore easier for the besiegers. Bernardo de Gálvez, however, publicly challenged the navy's courage and seamanship by personally sailing a ship into the harbor to show that it could be done. The navy then followed.[12] Later, to the chagrin of army officers, Charles III rewarded both services for the victory at Pensacola when the contribution of one seemed greater than the other. A substantial number of army and navy officers in Havana in 1782 were participants in all of these events.

Even foreign allies helped to make interservice matters worse. Solano's command at Havana was particularly recalcitrant in cooperating with its French counterpart in preparing for the attack on Jamaica. Undoubtedly this stemmed from the agreement designed by Saavedra in St. Domingue which put French troops under the command of Gálvez and Spanish ships under the directions of de Grasse. Such an accord was logical since most of the troops were Spanish and the bulk of the naval escort was French. However, Solano, no less than Gálvez, disliked serving under others, and at Pensacola he had commanded French ships in his armada. In the navy's view Saavedra had been too willing to make an arrangement which ensured the army would reap most of the glory coming from the Jamaican campaign. As a consequence Solano reluctantly supported the French and most certainly felt no urgency about finding ships for the New Providence campaign. Faced with a sluggish ally, French naval officials did not hide their contempt for Solano and his command.[13]

French disapproval of either branch of the Spanish military was unpleasant since the two countries were ruled by different branches of the same family. Yet it particularly grated on Bernardo de Gálvez in Havana. Bernardo and most Spanish army officers were Francophiles, modeling their service after what they considered the best land force in Europe, the French. Bernardo had even married into a French-speaking family in Louisiana. In constant contact with his French allies while preparing to move to the Cape, Gálvez had no excuse to offer for Solano, his fellow Spaniard. However, the admiral provided his own defense.

Solano made it clear that he exercised an independent command at Havana, not one under the jurisdiction of Indies or army officials. Saavedra's agreement with the French was not necessarily binding on him if he concluded that it interfered with the navy's responsibilities elsewhere. With some justification the admiral felt that he did not have enough ships to assist the French in covering St. Domingue, to defend the harbor of Havana from a surprise British attack, and to furnish escorts for forays such as that intended against New Providence. Without some minimal naval protection Cagigal could not launch an expedition against the Bahamas. To wait until Solano felt able to assign ships would probably mean that the attack on Nassau would never take place. Providentially, perhaps, the escort that Cagigal needed materialized in January 1782 from a most unexpected source, the rebellious English colonies. Commodore Alexander Gillon and his frigate, the *South Carolina*, sailed into the Havana harbor on 13 January.

The *South Carolina* was the largest and most powerful ship under American command during the war. She was part of the state navy of South Carolina, and only a series of bizarre and fortuitous circumstances brought this vessel to Cuba. Why this frigate happened to be in Havana and the reasons why Commodore Gillon agreed to participate in the New Providence expedition greatly influenced events in the forthcoming campaign against New Providence.

The *South Carolina* was still on her maiden voyage when she arrived at Havana in January. The frigate's cruise had begun five months earlier on 7 August 1781 from Texel in the Netherlands. On board the ship for her inaugural trip were twenty-six passengers, including some very prominent Americans of the era. John Adams, the American envoy to Holland, entrusted this ship to take his son Charles back to Massachusetts. John Trumbull (a noted New England painter), Benjamin Waterhouse (later a distinguished physician and scientist at Harvard), William Jackson (celebrated for his surviving notes on the Constitutional Convention), James Searle (a well-known Pennsylvanian), Joshua Barney (an important American sea captain), and William Brailsford (scion of a leading Charleston family) all took passage on this ship expecting a fast and safe trip home. They were to be disappointed.

The *South Carolina* was an impressive ship by any measure, mounting 40 cannons (the bulk being 36 pounders) and carrying a complement of nearly 550 men, over 300 of whom were marines. Her keel stretched 168 feet, and the vessel's draught reached 22 feet. Observers occasionally described the ship as a boat sporting the features of a 74–gun man-of-war.[14] There were very few frigates in any navy that could match the *South Carolina* in firepower. By comparison all other American vessels were dwarfed. The much more famous *Bonhomme Richard* under John Paul Jones, for example, carried a full complement of only 380 men and 40 guns (most of which were 12 pounders). By all rights the *South Carolina* cruise should have been one of the most distinguished American naval voyages of the Revolution, especially since this ship would lead the only successful American maritime expedition to seize and hold an entire enemy colony, the Bahamas. Instead, students of the American Revolution have for the most part ignored the *South Carolina*. For a ship so little known today, it is amazing how controversial the vessel was in her own time.[15]

Controversy and the *South Carolina* were synonymous from the moment its keel was laid in Holland. Commissioned by the French government, the frigate was originally intended for the American rebels. Because she was finished when Holland was still neutral, the Dutch refused to release the ship directly to the Americans. For reasons not clear but undoubtedly connected with French internal affairs, the court in Paris then turned the frigate over in 1780 to the chevalier, or prince, of Luxembourg, a member of the prominent Montmorency family. As a private citizen the chevalier might find some use for the ship that could harm the British and earn a profit at the same time. The chevalier decided to lease

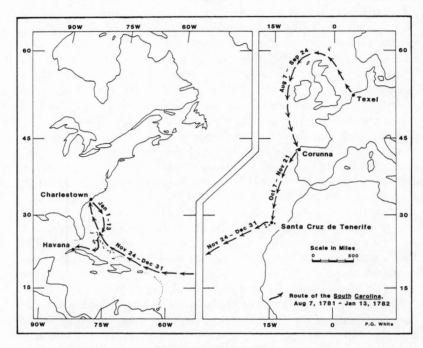

Map 1. North Atlantic

his new acquisition to anyone willing to pay for such a ship. There were any number of American sea captains roaming Europe looking for just such an opportunity. The lucky salt to get the prince's property was an agent for the state of South Carolina in Europe, Alexander Gillon of Charleston. Gillon held a commodore's commission from his home state. In 1780 he signed a three-year contract with the prince to take command of the new frigate, changing the name of the vessel from *L'Indien* to the *South Carolina*.

Precisely why the chevalier offered the lease to Gillon is unknown. There were a number of Americans who wanted the ship for themselves, including John Paul Jones. Gillon, however, had a number of advantages over his competitors. Although a prominent merchant in Charleston, he had been born in Holland and reared in a mixed Scottish-Dutch household. After migrating to the British colonies in 1766, he married a prominent widow in Charleston and earned himself a reputation early in the American Revolution as a partisan of the rebellion and one who knew much about the sea.[16] When those who favored a new order in South Carolina decided to send commissioners to Europe to bring back a state navy to defend the colony against British and loyalist marauders, Gillon was a logical choice to serve as a commissioner. He had friends and family across the ocean. He was also multilingual, speaking Dutch, French, English, and probably German. Gillon also had practical knowledge about gaining access to the courts of Europe and understood the importance of looking like a commodore, even though he had never commanded a warship. Gillon insisted on acquiring and wearing an impressive uniform. To some of his fellow Americans, several of whom were clearly envious, he looked ludicrous. These individuals were not, however, those whom Gillon had to influence.[17] Gillon, moreover, was a man of considerable commercial means who was willing to pledge his personal wealth as security in obtaining a frigate. On 30 May 1780, the prince and the commodore signed the contract for Gillon to command the *South Carolina*.

Terms of this agreement were very important because they would greatly influence how the commodore would use his ship. In return for a command that was to last three years, Gillon pledged to employ the ship to capture prizes, booty that would be sent to France for condemnation and sale. The chevalier did not want a fighting frigate, a factor that probably hurt John Paul Jones's chance of acquiring the vessel. The prince would receive one-fourth of the prize money, the rest being divided between the state of South Carolina (one-fourth) and the ship's crew (one-half). Upon the return of the *South Carolina* safely to Europe after three years the prince would receive a final payment of 100,000 livres. If the ship were lost during this time, Gillon and his state were obligated to pay an indemnity of 400,000 livres, three-quarters of which had to be in specie. The commodore also promised to compensate the prince if the ship were used for purposes other than scouring the sea for booty. As can be seen, there was an important business side to how the *South Carolina* could be employed. If the frigate did not make money from the war, Gillon and the state of South Carolina had a considerable debt to repay.[18]

Although the lease with the chevalier stated that the *South Carolina* must be put to sea within three months, the frigate did not leave Holland until August 1781. Getting the ship to sea was almost as hard as obtaining the vessel in the first place. Gillon worked diligently to enlist a crew from all possible sources. His naval officers were all Americans, including many South Carolinians, but the crew was a mixture of many nationalities, especially Americans, English, French, Dutch, Irish, and Germans.[19] The commodore recruited the American part of his crew from compatriots stranded in various continental ports, plus a substantial number of sailors who were exchanged or escaped from English prisons. Gillon's polyglot crew presented many problems, and there were deserters at every port of call.

The remaining manpower came from the three hundred marines who were a gift from the chevalier of Luxembourg. They were called variously the Legion of Luxembourg or the Volunteers of Luxembourg under the command of the chevalier D'Aubry. The prince of Luxembourg controlled several private armies during the war which he employed most notably against the Channel Islands and in the India Ocean. These legionnaires served for the adventure and increased profit that their prince provided them in comparison to duty with regular French forces. No man-of-war could survive without marines, and the slow arrival in Amsterdam of these so-called volunteers had much to do with Gillon's delayed departure.[20]

Other factors than the tardiness of the Luxembourg marines also slowed the commodore's departure. Provisioning the *South Carolina* was a massive problem, and Gillon had no public supply system to rely on. In order to outfit his ship the commodore borrowed heavily, promising to meet this debt in part by carrying cargo and escorting ships back to North America. Paying passengers were also a source of income. Yet the officers of the *South Carolina* were caught in a vicious circle. The longer the ship waited to sail, the harder it was to get new capital. Those who had already loaned money and goods to the commodore began to doubt that his ship would ever depart. Some creditors tried to recover their capital by seizing goods and even the ship itself before it was too late. Gillon was just a few steps ahead of these worried investors when he sailed in August. Unfortunately he was also a few steps ahead of several transports whose owners had expected an escort across the Atlantic by the commodore.[21]

Once at sea Gillon seemed to be indecisive about what to do. With such a large number of people aboard, the commodore had stores for only a modest time afloat, and he expended a considerable portion of these before losing sight of Holland. With fewer ships to escort than expected, he sailed north around Scotland looking for prizes, finally taking two.[22] His passengers certainly anticipated that the ship would head directly for the New World. Fearing that he did not have the supplies needed to cross the Atlantic, the commodore turned loose his small convoy and sailed south, putting in at Corunna, Spain, for provisions and minor repairs. In port he had to quell a violent mutiny by some of the French sailors.[23] There, also, a number of passengers left the ship in disgust and anger, feeling that this meandering Charlestonian never intended to reach the New World. One reportedly even challenged Gillon to a duel.[24] Complaints from these disgruntled passengers would cost Gillon dearly when he finally arrived in the United States.

Gillon spent nearly a month in Corunna taking on supplies. While in the Spanish port the commodore provoked controversy by allowing, or enticing, some Irish soldiers in Spanish service to desert and sign on his ship as sailors. This would not be the last time that the *South Carolina* recruited sailors from those already in the service of Spain. Nor was Gillon reluctant to take men bound to service with his own countrymen if the opportunity arose.[25] Even though the commodore could not pay for the assistance received in Corunna, adding to the trail of debt begun in Amsterdam, Spanish officials were obviously relieved to see the Charlestonian sail away. But the Spaniards had not seen the last of Gillon. On 1 November 1781 the *South Carolina* dropped anchor off Santa Cruz de Tenerife in the Canary Islands.

The commodore's penchant for Spanish ports had much to do with an earlier trip in 1778 when royal officials in Havana had assisted him generously as he traveled from South Carolina to Europe.[26] Spanish help to American rebels was extremely important during the war, particularly in such areas as finances, maritime supplies, and trade. Gillon's motive in stopping off at the Canaries was to receive some of this aid. A large number of his marines, nearly one-third of the Legion of Luxembourg, had become sick and needed immediate medical attention. The commodore persuaded the French consul at Santa Cruz to assist him in obtaining medical care for these legionnaires. Gillon also had on board a number of people, some sailors and several officers of the Legion of Luxembourg, who no longer had faith that the *South Carolina* was going to accomplish anything. Many wanted to get off the ship before she sailed too far from home. Those whom the commodore no longer desired aboard his ship and those who were too seriously ill to recuperate within a few days were left behind when the *South Carolina* slipped away from Santa Cruz at 2:00 A.M. on 24 November to avoid paying local debts. Gillon's disturbing habit of taking irregular leave of ports greatly embarrassed the helpful French consul in the Canaries. He now had to find a way to pay the medical expenses of many countrymen discarded by the commodore. The Spanish governor also took offense at Gillon's unorthodox approach to financial obligations.[27]

Gillon pointed his ship for home and arrived off Charleston on 31 December 1781. It had been over three years since the commodore had departed his state, and the events in the southern colonies had changed dramatically since then. Gillon entered the Charleston channel cautiously, approached the port close enough to see the houses of the town, noticed that the city was in enemy hands, and attracted the attention of several British men-of-war, which gave brief chase. He turned his ship around and sailed for the open sea. With such a large company he needed a friendly port to resupply, and the *South Carolina* badly needed repairs—she leaked and the main mast was sprung. This time a third Spanish port beckoned—Havana. Why he did not head north to an American city such as Philadelphia or Boston can only be conjectured. Certainly the winter season made northern sailing hazardous. Possibly he foresaw an unfriendly welcome awaiting him in the north.

At any rate the *South Carolina* headed south. In passage she took a risky route to the Cuban capital, sailing through the Gulf of Providence. Once in the Old Bahama Channel the frigate ran across a small Jamaican convoy of five merchant ships on its way to Scotland. Gillon captured all five and took these prizes with him to Havana.[28] Any ship with prizes was most welcome in Cuba, for the sale of these captured vessels meant that Gillon could pay for his supplies in hard cash. Yet the *South Carolina* received more hospitality than she might have merited otherwise because she could now provide what the Spanish navy chose not to, an armed escort for Cagigal to Nassau. The disjointed pieces that would make up the expedition against New Providence had now come together.

Chapter Two

THE EXPEDITION TRIUMPHANT

Before January 1782 Commodore Gillon and General Cagigal had not anticipated working together. Indeed, these two gentlemen were not acquainted nor aware of the other's existence. Who first broached the possibility of a joint expedition against the Bahamas is not clear from the surviving records. American sources indicate that Cagigal approached Gillon about the project, and this is logical in light of the general's needs. Yet the captain general's papers claim the opposite. Unlikely as it may seem because of the Spanish service rivalries, Admiral Solano might have originated the idea of using Gillon. With so many postwar factors coloring memories of the event, the truth can not be determined. Whatever the source, however, both sides quickly realized the mutual benefits that a co-operative venture against the Bahamas could bring.[1]

A short expedition such as the one planned against New Providence did not need a sizable escort. The success of this type of campaign depended upon the element of surprise; moreover, the *South Carolina* was bigger than any likely foe between Havana and Nassau. The British admiralty refused to station a large man-of-war permanently in the Bahamas because the shallow waters of the archipelago made Nassau a dangerous anchorage for ships with considerable draughts. By adding some American and Spanish privateers present in Havana, Gillon could provide the New Providence expedition with adequate protection. Bernardo de Gálvez, still in Havana preparing for his departure to the Cape

18

when the American frigate arrived, approved of using the *South Carolina* against Nassau. Accompanied by Cuban dignitaries he even inspected the ship, admiring her armament and design. Admiral Solano corresponded with the commodore and knew that the *South Carolina* would shield Cagigal's convoy.[2] After the campaign Gálvez and Solano denied any prior knowledge about Cagigal's agreement to employ the American frigate or any other foreigners against the Bahamas, a remarkable loss of memory that their own correspondence does not support.

Until the end of April 1781 Cagigal and Gillon worked diligently to launch their expedition. The actual plans for the attack had been completed the year before by Luis Huet, and most attention centered upon supplies, ships, and men. The two leaders were under considerable pressure to act rapidly. The upcoming assault on Jamaica loomed on the horizon, and Gálvez expected Cagigal and his small army to be at the Cape in time to participate. If the captain general and commodore procrastinated too long, Gálvez would have to cancel the expedition against New Providence, something that he did try to do in April after de Grasse sent word that the French fleet was about to arrive.[3] Gillon also could not afford to dally with his powerful ship in Havana. His contract with the chevalier de Luxembourg had only a little more than a year to run, and inactivity was an expensive luxury.

There were other pressures to expedite the attack on New Providence. As soon as Gillon and Cagigal had agreed on the project, port officials in Havana clamped an embargo on all ships leaving the harbor. In order to keep the expedition secret no merchant vessel of any kind, not even a fishing boat, could depart until the fleet had sailed. Although secrecy was the main purpose of the embargo, a closed port served another function by convincing captains whose ships sat idle to volunteer for convoy service. Sea captains and merchants could hardly make money sitting at anchor in Havana, but they could earn income by contracting with the Spanish exchequer to transport troops to New Providence and by acting as armed privateers. Cuban officials sweetened participation in the fleet by allowing these vessels to start toward their home ports ahead of those embargoed in Havana. Yet even those not sailing with the expedition clamored for the convoy to leave promptly so they could soon get on with the business of buying and selling merchandise.[4]

In spite of the pressure to sail a host of unexpected problems conspired to delay the departure date. The Spanish forces moving to the Cape under Bernardo de Gálvez had first priority on most goods and services in Havana. Until this much larger operation completely cleared Havana, officials gave only secondary attention to the Bahamian endeavor.[5] Nevertheless, Cagigal's army was ready to sail by February. Gillon's navy was not.

The commodore found numerous reasons to stay put. Once committed to the expedition the American had second thoughts about his ability to direct and protect such a large convoy. He had never undertaken such a project. His understandable caution was reinforced by sundry requirements to make the *South Carolina* ready for this project. At no point since the frigate's fitting out in Holland in 1781, if indeed then, had the *South Carolina* ever been made completely seaworthy. Havana provided an excellent opportunity to correct these deficiencies.

Another major shortcoming of the *South Carolina* was her diminished crew. Plagued by an inability to pay his men and by unforeseen conflicts between French marines and American sailors, Gillon had seen his ship muster decline seriously after reaching Cuba. In February alone over eighty hands deserted in Havana, nearly twenty percent of his manpower. This was nothing new for Gillon; he had experienced a loss of marines and sailors at every port on the way to Havana. But the Havana stay was much longer. There were many American merchant ships in port which were short of crew and whose captains offered good wages, caring little where their recruits came from.

As a result Gillon took extraordinary measures to acquire more hands for his ship, one of which involved encouraging Dutch and German-speaking soldiers to desert their Spanish regiments. The commodore's ledger even had an entry for bonuses (or bribes) paid to these new recruits. At one point Gillon's residence in Havana was full of discarded Spanish army uniforms from crew members who had changed their military garb for that of Gillon's sailors. His newest seamen occasionally embarrassed the commodore by jeering at former comrades when outbound regiments aboard Spanish ships happened to pass close to the anchored *South Carolina*. Gillon's search for sailors even reached into the ranks of German-speaking British soldiers who had been captured at Pensacola and were in Havana awaiting exchange. Had Spanish officials not needed the commodore for the New Providence expedi-

tion, his recruiting activities would surely have caused his welcome
in Havana to wear thin.[6]

On 22 April the expedition headed for sea. Cagigal and Gillon
had assembled a fleet of some fifty-nine vessels, twelve of which
were American merchantmen fitted out as armed privateers. With
the addition of the *South Carolina* the total number of American
ships rose to thirteen.[7] Altogether the convoy mounted an impressive 311 guns. The fleet counted 1,531 sailors, along with 2,000
soldiers in the Cagigal units.[8] Because of uncooperative winds it
took the expedition nearly a week to clear the harbor in Havana
and to sail beyond sight of the city. The ever-jittery commodore,
fearful that the slow pace would destroy the expedition's secrecy,
increased the size of the convoy by impounding some Spanish truce
ships headed for Charleston which had tried to sail past his fleet.

By 30 April 1782 Gillon had sighted Matanzas and had begun
navigating up the Bahama Channel. The commodore divided the
convoy into three squadrons with orders to travel during the day
and to anchor at night. The fleet had no trouble finding its way
since its pilots were residents of the Bahamas, the same helmsmen
who had guided an American raid against the islands in 1776.[9]
For the Spaniards these Bahamian pilots promised sweet revenge,
since it had been Bahamians who steered the British to Havana
in 1762. On 2 May the convoy reached the Biminis and turned
east. En route Gillon's fleet sighted, and was sighted by, numerous
ships. The convoy captured three small vessels recently departed
from Nassau. Intelligence from these prizes indicated that British
officials on New Providence were worried about the possibility of
a Spanish strike and that some reinforcements had recently arrived
from Charleston. Yet this same intelligence also revealed that the
colony had no recent warning that it was about to be attacked.
On the evening of 5 May the convoy rested off the harbor of Nassau.[10]

Before they deployed to invade Nassau, however, cooperation
between the two attacking allies was unexpectedly strained to the
breaking point. In spite of Spanish plans to launch an immediate
attack Gillon instructed all ships to remain at anchor and await
his orders before moving against the British. For a moment, consequently, Gillon and Cagigal came to view each other instead of
the British as the adversary. Indeed, Cagigal and the entire command of the Spanish army feared momentarily that the commo-

dore intended to hold them hostage aboard the *South Carolina*, which was serving as Cagigal's flagship. With the Spanish army divided among dozens of transports and with Cagigal and his staff isolated on the frigate, Gillon and his three hundred marines could have easily done this if it were his wish. To understand this surprising turn of events it is necessary to look at a variety of attitudes, personalities, and earlier war experiences that converged upon the convoy at anchor.

The agreement that had been struck between Cagigal and Gillon in January 1782 had been unwritten and could be, in good faith, interpreted in several contradictory ways. Just how contradictory became suddenly apparent on 5 May. In the eyes of Cagigal and his staff, this was a Spanish expedition—planned, organized, and run by officers serving Charles III. The participating Americans were, at best, auxiliaries or, at worst, hired help. Indeed, the exchequer in Havana had signed contracts with all but two of the American vessels (the *South Carolina* was one of the exceptions) stipulating how much compensation each American captain would receive and what service each was expected to perform in return. In addition, the Spanish treasury had furnished all the American participants other aid as well.

In spite of this financial assistance Gillon viewed the New Providence expedition as a joint endeavor by two opponents of Great Britain.[11] The American contribution was undoubtedly the lesser, but it was indispensable. Without it there would not have been an attack on the Bahamas. Gillon, consequently, expected a role in the capitulation negotiations with the British as befitted an equal partner, and he also expected a substantial share of the spoils of war. The commodore had assumed that Cagigal would take charge of the booty seized on land and that Gillon would supervise that captured afloat in the harbor.[12] Considering the maritime wealth of the Bahamian merchants, the commodore's assumptions might not have been the fairest division of prizes. But Gillon was not the only person interested in making money from the war. An exclusively Spanish expedition meant that there would be no need to divide the victor's profits with the Americans, and Cagigal had no intentions of sharing with Gillon or anyone else. The Spaniards envisioned no role for the commodore in the expedition beyond providing the sea escort. As unlikely as it seems, these crucial issues had not been discussed beforehand—but they were now.[13]

Nerves and additional financial worries also played a role in

Gillon's behavior at this point. Nassau and its environs did not provide a safe anchorage for a man-of-war the size of the *South Carolina*. The British had always considered this port unsuitable for stationing large ships, and now Gillon agreed. Moreover, information garnered from the ships taken while approaching New Providence indicated that the Spanish convoy had just missed a small British flotilla returning to Charleston from Nassau that had been escorted by several frigates close to the size of the *South Carolina*. There was no telling when the bad weather would expose the *South Carolina* to serious danger or when another escorted enemy fleet might appear. Already a jittery commander because of unfamiliar responsibilities in leading such a large convoy, Gillon found new anxieties over the weather and the British, which caused him to demand that his ship be insured for 300,000 pesos and that he be paid some 60,000 pesos in costs. The time to arrange such matters was obviously not when battle was imminent, but it must be kept in mind that Gillon had a binding contract with the chevalier of Luxembourg to produce money with the *South Carolina* and that he had volunteered his own property and wealth as collateral should the ship be lost or misused. So fearful did Spanish officials become that Gillon intended to satisfy his financial request by seizing the funds brought along to support the expedition that they conspired to sneak the king's coffers off the *South Carolina*. Perhaps a bit too smugly, Spanish officials assumed that help in selling Gillon's Jamaican prizes in Havana plus the assistance in outfitting and manning the *South Carolina* were payment enough.[14]

There was yet another unexpected and personal problem upon sighting Nassau. As befitted a prominent Charlestonian merchant whose business connections before the war had reached across the Atlantic, Gillon spoke many languages, Dutch and English being his native tongues. But the commodore did not speak Spanish. General Cagigal, on the other hand, had only his native Castilian and a limited command of French. As a result Gillon and Cagigal had to communicate through an interpreter. There certainly was no shortage of Spaniards who spoke English, particularly in Havana with its long-standing commercial ties to surrounding English colonies. Moreover, an old tradition of the Spanish army fielding Irish units and employing Irish officers still functioned; many such persons were assigned to Havana.[15]

Nevertheless, the most convenient translator for the two commanders was Francisco de Miranda, Cagigal's aide-de-camp. Miranda would gain fame later as one of the principal leaders for independence in Spanish America. He was, however, no rebel at this time but rather a very ambitious junior officer in the Spanish army. It was possible for one to rise in rank in the Spanish army on merit alone, but opportunities to prove one's mettle did not come frequently in the military, even during wartime. It was far more common to move up in rank through the influence of powerful friends and relatives. Miranda, who was sensitive and very intelligent, had linked his career to the coattails of Cagigal sometime in the late 1770s. Until the New Providence expedition this had proven to be a wise decision. Through the good graces of the captain general Miranda had jumped in rank from captain to lieutenant colonel (ahead of most officers of similar age and experience) in the space of four years. Cagigal came to trust Miranda completely and stubbornly risked his career later for his aide-de-camp.[16]

The bond that was so strong between the captain general and his aide-de-camp did not, however, exist between the commodore and Miranda. While still in Havana Gillon and Miranda had frequent dealings in preparing the expedition, and Gillon occasionally addressed letters to Cagigal's aide-de-camp as "my friend."[17] Yet the last-minute hitches before the campaign caused the two men to lose patience with each other. Both soon reached the point of portraying the other in the worst possible light in their messages to Cagigal. The commodore's apparent demand that Miranda be dismissed from the expedition brought a vitriolic reply from Cagigal (although almost certainly written by Miranda himself) that described Gillon's letter as one full of "deceits, falsehoods, insolences, and audacities" and warning him not to broach the subject of Miranda again.[18] This was extremely strong language by eighteenth century standards, particularly between allies. Although Cagigal would eventually have kinder words to say about the commodore, the intense dislike between Gillon and Miranda never disappeared.[19] The commodore's increasing animosity and unpredictability had much to do with Cagigal's decision to debark from the South Carolina just as fast as he could. Miranda had convinced him that the American leader could not be trusted.

One last difficulty emerged that had its roots in the nature of the struggle against the British. Unlike the French Bourbons, Charles III never officially recognized the American rebels as a government or as an ally. Indeed, the Spanish attitude toward the

American cause could best be described as one of uneasy tolerance but not approval. For the most part American officials accepted this Spanish posture out of necessity. They needed Spanish assistance too much to insist upon recognition or approbation.

Now and then, however, Spain's refusal to consider the Americans as allies resulted in awkward moments. At the conquest of Pensacola, for example, the victorious Spaniards paroled most of the captured British garrison, forbidding those soldiers from fighting against Spain or its allies until a proper exchange could be arranged. Yet Spain and the Thirteen Colonies were not officially allied. Theoretically, hence, the parolees could fight the Americans, and they did. Many of the Pensacola captives were sent off to New York, in the eyes of the Spaniards the least harmful post to deposit them. The British commanders promptly integrated them into the ranks facing the besieging Americans. Fearing a repetition of what had happened in West Florida, Gillon made it clear in his correspondence to Cagigal and Miranda, both of whom had been at Pensacola and were oblivious to American sensitivities on this point, that he would not accept any surrender that allowed the British forces in the Bahamas to be transported to a mainland port where they could fight against Gillon's fellow rebels. Although not willing to allow the commodore to participate as an equal in the campaign, Cagigal recognized the merit of this complaint by Gillon and indicated his willingness to satisfy it.[20]

The confrontation between the two allies lasted less than twenty-four hours. It was Gillon who backed down and allowed a united front to be presented to the British. Why the mercurial Gillon relented in his demands is uncertain, but Cagigal and his staff had even discussed the possibility of landing the entire Spanish army on a nearby island, fortifying themselves there, and writing an urgent appeal to Bernardo de Gálvez at the Cape for ships to take Gillon's place in blockading the port. The Spanish command also toyed with the idea of holding two surrender ceremonies, a bogus proceeding in which the American commodore could sign anything that he wanted and a second in which there would be no Americans present. Just how tight-lipped the British would have been during these two functions can only be surmised. Gillon later claimed that the controversy ended when Cagigal verbally agreed to his requests, particularly those involving money.[21]

Perhaps much of the reason that the confrontation went no further was that the commodore may well have been surprised at how seriously the Spaniards had reacted to his litany of demands. Should the expedition fail because of this dispute, the commodore would have been saddled with the blame, and he did not need this burden on top of many other difficulties facing his return home. Gillon might have also been influenced to yield when he realized that the Spaniards had removed all their officers from the *South Carolina*, which had been Cagigal's flagship, to Spanish transports in the harbor. Whether he seriously entertained the prospect of holding the Spanish command hostage is doubtful, but once this possibility was gone, the commodore lost what leverage he had. At any rate, the allies started their maneuvers the next day, 6 May. Their private squabble was over, although not forgotten.

In Nassau itself British governor John Maxwell was unaware of the dispute among his foes in the harbor, sensing it only later when it was long past the point where it might have been useful to him. Since assuming his post in 1781 Maxwell had always feared the worst for his colony in the form of an attack by the Spaniards. Now it was a reality. He attempted to send a ship to Charleston with a description of the Spanish forces and a belated appeal for help, but essentially Maxwell was unprepared for something that was his duty to anticipate. British intelligence had repeatedly warned Maxwell that an attack was likely, but no one had really planned a defense.[22] To a great extent this lack of preparedness could be accounted for by earlier Bahamian experiences with the war.

Although New Providence would earn the reputation after the war as a colony that was a loyalist bastion within the empire, such was not the case during the American Revolution. New Providence was a vulnerable and deeply divided British colony from the moment fighting began in 1775. Close geographically to the mainland colonies and also dependent upon these nearby possessions for trade, the island had an important faction which sympathized with the rebellion. There were many others in the Bahamas who did not care which side won. Island loyalty would swing to whichever side seized power.

The Americans had twice raided the islands during the war, once in 1776 under the command of Ezekiel Hopkins and a second time in 1778 under the direction of John Peck Rathburne. In both cases the rebels occupied Nassau with no resistance, had been welcomed and feted by leading residents of the capital, and had left with considerable war booty. Governor Maxwell saw no reason to disagree with the assessment of his predecessor, Montfort Browne, that the islands were full of rebel sympathizers.[23] Had these earlier raiders come to stay rather than loot, New Providence could have easily been the fourteenth colony.

Since the Spaniards did come with serious intentions of remaining, the most significant divisions on the islands were among the governing elite loyal to England. Most of these cleavages were common to other English colonies. Their intensity, however, may have had a peculiar Bahamian twist. In the 1770s a dangerous split between the islands' governors and council occurred. This political tiff initially grew out of a power vacuum created by an absentee governor and the existence of an ambitious council.

Montfort Browne, governor of the colony when the war started, came to the Bahamas in 1774. Once secure in his new position, Browne sought in every way possible to keep his appointment and salary while not being physically present in Nassau. During his initial term as governor (1774–76) he spent much of his time in West Florida, where he had extensive investments in land, returning to his Caribbean post in time to be captured by the first American raiding party in 1776. Sent to the mainland as a prisoner and then exchanged, Browne chose to occupy his next two years serving as a provincial officer in New York City, resisting repeated attempts by the Colonial Office to return him to his vacant post in Nassau.

When finally threatened with the loss of his appointment, Browne sailed to Nassau in December 1778 only to find that most of his patronage positions had been taken away by the lieutenant governor and council in his absence. Those who had lost their jobs now expected to regain them, and those who had in the meantime received posts feared they would lose them. Because of Browne's bitter memories of 1776, when he tried unsuccessfully to organize resistance against the Americans, and also because of his years spent with loyalist units in New York, he returned to the Caribbean obsessed with questions of treason, suspecting most Bahamians of being openly or furtively supportive of the rebellion.

Browne, whose skills as a politician were somewhat crude, made no secret of his opinions about local fealty to George III. He demanded that everyone, particularly those on the council and in public positions, sign loyalty pledges. This contest over government jobs and over who could best demonstrate their patriotism resulted in a paper war between Browne and the council, paralyzing public activities in all areas including defense. The general assembly in Nassau even went to the extent of appropriating tax funds to bring charges against the governor in London. It was not until this dispute forced the court to recall Governor Browne in 1780 that much attention could be given to military affairs.[24] Yet Maxwell, Browne's replacement, also had to be very careful in his dealings with the council. Fresh from one victory over a former governor, council members were not about to surrender authority to a new one.[25]

Unfortunately the governor-council dispute was not the only internal squabble paralyzing the government. The two top military officials on New Providence in the late 1770s—Governor Browne and Captain John Grant—were bitter rivals. Because the colony's militia had shown itself singularly unable or unwilling to fight against American marauders in 1776 and 1778, Browne brought back with him several companies of garrison soldiers, invalids no longer fit for a field campaign but competent to man the colony's forts. Browne held a high rank (brigadier general) in the British army and, as governor, was the chief military officer in the colony. Nevertheless, the commandant of the garrison, contemptuous of any person in a civilian position and personally hostile to Browne, refused to acknowledge the governor's authority in any military matter. So intense did this dispute become over who exercised supreme military control in the Bahamas that both men and their followers feared violence in the streets of Nassau from the other faction.

When Maxwell arrived in Nassau, this problem continued and was not resolved until late 1780, when Captain Grant was finally recalled to New York.[26] Until that time cooperation among the leading British officials in the Bahamas on how to defend the colony had been nonexistent. After that time, with cooperation finally possible, plans were still not developed. Certainly Governor Maxwell had the responsibility for doing so. By then Maxwell had evidently reached the conclusion that New Providence could not defend itself. Only the presence of major assistance from outside could make the colony's defenses viable. Such a position relegated the governor's military efforts to begging for troops from British officials, and it conveniently shifted accountability to others for what might happen militarily to the Bahamas. Regardless of where the blame rests, the political divisions which afflicted the ruling elite of the islands continued to play a crucial role in Bahamian events after the islands were occupied by Spain and even later when British rule returned in April 1783.

As unprepared as Governor Maxwell was on 6 May 1782, he was not completely helpless. With maximum participation he could call upon enough regulars, militia, and sailors from local privateers to raise a force numbering approximately 1,400 men, well over half the size of the attackers.[27] Operating on the defensive, Maxwell hardly faced hopeless odds. Furthermore, the Gillon-Cagigal imbroglio in the harbor gave the governor a little time to mobilize his forces. Maxwell, however, lacked the will to fight. So did the other civilian leaders of the colony. The governor and others responsible for the defense of Nassau later explained their willingness to strike their colors without a struggle as the only logical decision for a garrison so overwhelmingly outnumbered—a perception of the enemy's strength that was incorrect. The governor noted that influential figures on the island urged him to avoid useless expenditure of life and property.[28] A judicious mixture of Spanish bluster and moderation was also a factor in the decision not to fight.

In Cagigal's initial communications with Maxwell the Spanish commander warned the British that any resistance would expose Nassau and its residents to the fortunes of war, with the Spaniards deciding unilaterally what constituted booty. Merchants composed an important element in Nassau and in the militia. They hardly favored even token resistance if it meant placing their property at the whim of the enemy. Even more critical, however, was the promise from Cagigal that a quick surrender would result only in the confiscation of public property and private weapons of war. Merchants could continue doing business as usual under British laws and taxation. Even privateers, one of the principal reasons for the Spanish seizure of the colony, would remain in their owners' hands, although they would now have to be turned to peaceful purposes. The basic changes would be a Spanish governor, a small foreign garrison, and a different flag flying over Nassau's forts.

These were remarkably generous surrender terms, and the quarrel between the Spaniards and the Americans determined their composition. Uncertain about Commodore Gillon, Captain General Cagigal wanted a quick and painless victory. Later, exchequer officials in Havana would criticize the mild terms of capitulation by noting that the fruits of victory in New Providence did not even cover the costs of the expedition. Nevertheless, Bahamians found it to their advantage to give up rather than to fight. Maxwell notified the Spaniards on 7 May that he would surrender. He signed the capitulation agreement on 8 May.[29]

With relatively little property changing hands, and that mostly ashore in the form of weapons and public buildings, Gillon's prospects for booty disappeared. Whatever reward there might be for his participation in the expedition would have to come from the Spanish treasury back in Havana, a source of compensation that was no longer possible given his spat with the captain general. The commodore no longer pushed his demands and assisted the Spanish army by patrolling the sea-lanes around Nassau looking for hostile privateers. Nevertheless, he exacted a punishment of sorts for the misunderstandings that had occurred.

Gillon informed Cagigal that he now planned to depart shortly for the United States and would not escort Cagigal's troops back to Havana or to Cape François, where Bernardo de Gálvez awaited their arrival at any moment. Moreover, he insisted that none of the other American armed ships, some twelve to thirteen in number, be impressed to perform this service against their will. Since all the major escort vessels except one had been American, the loss of these ships, particularly the *South Carolina*, would leave New Providence and any returning fleet open to attack from the smallest of armed ships, exactly the type of vessels that abounded in the waters of the Bahamas. All of the American privateers carried commercial cargoes from Havana and never intended to return to Havana or to travel to the Cape after the fall of Nassau anyway. Nor had Cagigal expected them to do so. But the Spanish commander had counted upon the *South Carolina* remaining with the expedition until the end.[30] Cagigal had no choice but to accept this unilateral change of plans, but neither he nor the American commodore could really foresee what a heavy price Gillon's departure meant for their careers.

Chapter Three

VICTORS VANQUISHED

O n 14 May 1782 the *South Carolina*, and the American ships
that wished to leave, sailed from New Providence. After patrolling
a few days in Northwest Providence Channel this small fleet, heavily armed by American standards, headed for the Chesapeake and
Delaware Bays. The commodore dropped off dispatches first along
the South Carolina coast.[1] Although at least one boat from this
fleet put in at Baltimore, Gillon and most of his charges continued
on to Philadelphia, arriving by the end of May. They brought welcome news about the conquest of New Providence. Equally important for Philadelphia, merchant capital of the Confederation,
Gillon's ships carried word that the embargo at Havana had
ended.[2] The lucrative wartime trade with Cuba could resume.
Gillon's career as a commodore, however, was now almost over.

Circumstances had forced Gillon to put in at the wrong American port. It is difficult to see where else he might have gone in
May 1782 for Charleston was still in British hands and Havana
most certainly would not have welcomed him back. The southern
sea captain had few friends and numerous detractors in Philadelphia. Moreover, he had arrived empty-handed; no prizes trailed
his wake. Gillon was in a situation where the mere news of participation in a significant American naval victory was not enough.
He needed the booty that went with sea victories.

Gillon's contract with the chevalier de Luxembourg, requiring
that glory be coupled with financial gain, still hung over his head.

31

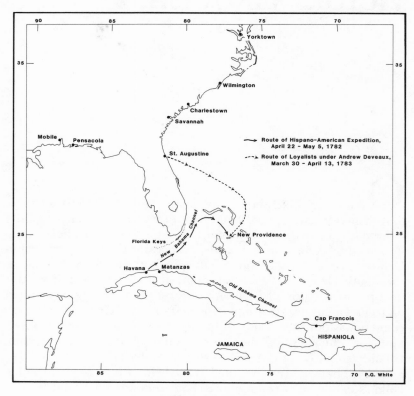

Map 2. Northern Caribbean

The French owner had long since grown nervous about the commodore's failure to funnel income back to France and wanted an accounting. In fact, the chevalier no longer trusted the commodore and wanted Gillon removed from command. Although an ocean separated the chevalier from Gillon, Philadelphia was one city where Gillon could not keep his ship. Working through the French government, Luxembourg had the French envoy in Philadelphia, the chevalier de la Luzerne, use his powerful influence with the new American government to prevent Gillon from sailing again on the *South Carolina*. There was no port in the Thirteen Colonies where French wishes exercised more sway than in the seat of the Confederation, Philadelphia.[3]

If French hostility were not enough, Commodore Gillon also had to face a host of personal enemies in Philadelphia who had not forgiven him for the manner in which he had acquired the *South Carolina* and the fashion in which this vessel had left Europe a year earlier. These antagonists, particularly William Jackson and James Searle (both passengers on the *South Carolina* when she left Texel), attacked Gillon publicly in the press and privately within the government.[4] Robert Morris, the important American minister of finance and a native of Philadelphia, took a dislike to the cavalier business methods of the commodore and worked to block the Charlestonian from returning immediately to sea. Gillon believed that Morris wanted his ship turned over to John Paul Jones, already the recipient of better public relations than Gillon, and reports of a duel between the commodore and Morris circulated in Philadelphia. Politically, Gillon did not have the clout to keep command of his ship in this city.[5]

When the *South Carolina* next left port, Gillon was not aboard. Instead, the Charlestonian was on his way home, where he would struggle for the rest of his life against relentless creditors who wanted payment for the obligations resulting from his naval command. Yet the commodore did not completely lose control of his ship. He relinquished command of the frigate to his subordinate officer throughout the voyage from Europe, Captain John Joyner, a fellow South Carolinian. To a limited degree fate was actually kind to Gillon. Joyner's last cruise in November 1782 was ill-starred. Only a few days out of port the American frigate met three British men-of-war off New York and struck her colors after a brief but bloody chase. This was the only time during the war that the considerable firepower of the *South Carolina* was used on an enemy, and the frigate apparently defended her honor well. Had Gillon been personally in charge at this point, it is unlikely that he could have returned home with any dignity. As it was, Joyner had to face a court-martial in his native state after the war for surrendering the frigate. A board of naval officers acquitted Joyner. It might not have done the same for Gillon.[6] As fickle as the fortunes of war and history were for the commodore, the Charlestonian's fate was certainly better than that of his erstwhile comrade-in-arms in New Providence, Juan Manuel de Cagigal.

The abandoned Spanish army and transport ships were about to sail into choppy waters of their own. No European country had an older claim to the Bahamas than did Spain, and the surrender of Governor Maxwell on 8 May had returned these islands to the control of the nation for whom Columbus had claimed them nearly three centuries earlier. Yet Spanish rule in 1782 began in a troubled fashion. It took the captain general several weeks to organize the occupation of New Providence, to set up an island government, to send Maxwell and his garrison regulars to England, and to plan the return trip to Havana (a task that should have fallen to Gillon). Since he was still the governor of Havana and also under orders to move part of his troops to the Cape, Cagigal hurried to return home and to communicate with Bernardo de Gálvez, who was preparing for the assault on Jamaica. Cagigal dispatched a ship to Havana with news of the victory and sent another vessel to Cape François with the same information. He decided to take all his forces to Havana as soon as it was feasible. There, transportation to the Cape would be available for the troops that were scheduled to join Gálvez. With this plan in mind, the captain general sailed for Cuba with part of his forces, leaving Brigadier General José Mannrique, his second in command, with orders to follow promptly with the rest of the original convoy. Unbeknownst to Cagigal, there would be no hero's welcome awaiting him in Havana or at the Cape. The shoals of Spanish bureaucratic politics were about to wreck his career.

In the long run the most serious trouble for Cagigal was at the Cape with the Spanish expeditionary army under Bernardo de Gálvez. Unexpectedly, the French fleet under Admiral de Grasse had suffered a disastrous defeat at the Battle of the Saints in April 1782. This setback postponed the allied assault upon Jamaica for another year, and ultimately indefinitely. Condemned to an unwanted and frustrating inactivity, the Spanish army at the Cape resentfully discovered that intended sideshows such as the attack on New Providence and the sweep along the Mosquito Coast moved to center stage. It had certainly not been the plan of Bernardo de Gálvez to command while others performed, and he had great difficulty mustering generous enthusiasm for the triumph of his subordinate, Cagigal.

To make matters worse, the messenger bringing the news of the New Providence victory to the Cape was Francisco de Miranda, Cagigal's aide-de-camp. As the most significant member of Cagigal's staff, although not the highest ranking, Miranda would normally have been a logical choice to perform such a task. In this case, however, Cagigal would have been better served by almost anyone else. To understand why, it is necessary to take another look at wartime Havana.

In the brief time that Miranda had served at Cagigal's side in Cuba, he had provoked the enmity of several powerful officials, most notably José de Solano, admiral of the fleet stationed in the Caribbean, and Juan Ignacio de Urriza, an influential intendant of the exchequer. Deep in the labyrinth of bureaucratic politics, Miranda had made himself extremely vulnerable to both men through the same incident. In 1781 Cagigal had sent Miranda to Jamaica under a flag of truce, ostensibly to bring back numerous Spanish prisoners of war confined on that island. The real reason for his visit, however, was espionage, to collect information about the defenses of the island in preparation for the Franco-Hispanic attack planned for the following year. Using truce ships for such purposes was a game that all sides played adroitly during the American Revolution, and Miranda came back with an impressive amount of military information and maps. As a result there was not much about Jamaica's defenses that the Spaniards did not know.

Such an intelligence assignment, moreover, was considered desirable duty because there was a financial reward for this work. It was a perfect cover for illegal trade. The actual exchange of prisoners could be completed in a few days, but good intelligence work took much longer. The eyes and ears of Miranda in Kingston would be English businessmen who would collect all types of information in return for a sales contract with Miranda, who paid for goods in hard currency. Conversely, the English did the same with the merchant community of Havana. Miranda had instructions from Cagigal to purchase scarce nautical supplies for Havana, and he had numerous orders from private citizens for other goods. Needless to say, there was obviously a healthy profit in this for Miranda, just as there had been for other Spaniards who had done this work before.

Although common practice in the Caribbean (and one has to suspect elsewhere as well), such spying techniques were not necessarily official state policy. It was hard for a government to punish illegal trading by private citizens yet support and condone it by military officers. When brought to the attention of the king and his council in Spain in the wrong way, contraband trade under any guise could be highly embarrassing. Upon his return from Jamaica at the end of his mission, Miranda saw one of his ships laden with illegal goods seized by the Spanish *guarda costa* (coast guard). Officials of the coast guard condemned Miranda's cargo as contraband, entitling these diligent officers to a high percentage of the value of these illegal goods. The *guarda costa*, which certainly operated on inside information in this case, was ultimately under the command of Solano, and the admiral knew the rules of espionage in the Caribbean. He was, however, in no mood to give any army officer a break. Furthermore, Solano knew full well that Miranda was linked directly to Cagigal and ultimately to Bernardo de Gálvez. The admiral could self-righteously raise the question whether intelligence or personal wealth was the principal objective of Miranda's visit to Kingston. Angered by the navy's action, the captain general forcibly removed the goods from *guarda costa* custody and protected Miranda for a while.

But slipping past the navy placed Cagigal's aide-de-camp at the mercy of the intendancy on shore. The nature of Spanish government in Cuba caused those who collected money, the intendancy, to be constantly at loggerheads with those who spent the funds, principally the captain general. From the viewpoint of the intendancy other officials on the island never appreciated its heroic efforts to secure money and often misused what was given them. For the captaincy general the exchequer was far too niggardly with what it had and insisted upon all types of onerous accounting practices designed to give the exchequer power to run the government. Like Solano, Urriza understood the rules of espionage, but he had little love for Cagigal, whose ties to the Gálvez family threatened to diminish the intendant's own connections with the clan.

Miranda's arrival from Jamaica with contraband goods presented the intendant with a wonderful opportunity to weaken the captain general's position. His tax officials were instructed to hold Miranda's illegal goods until some guidelines on what to do with this merchandise could be obtained from Spain. This was precisely the type of information that Cagigal did not want relayed across the ocean. Once again an even angrier Cagigal found it necessary to rescue Miranda and his goods from the clutches of a rival bureaucrat's control.[7]

If Solano and Urriza were not enough for any minor official to tangle with, Miranda also played a peripheral role in an affair that raised questions about the integrity of the Gálvez family. The highest ranking prisoner in Havana during the war was Major General John Campbell, the former commander of British forces at Pensacola. While in Cuba, Campbell challenged Gálvez's honor as an officer, charging that the Spanish general had violated the surrender agreements by deliberately slowing down the exchange of officers. Indeed, in some cases Gálvez refused to exchange certain British prisoners at all. Good Scotsman that he was, the British commander did not hide his resentment of Gálvez, penning a letter to the Spanish general which complained about ill treatment, calling into question the Spaniard's qualities as a gentleman, and maintaining that the only decent care Campbell received as a prisoner was from Cagigal.[8]

During General Campbell's captivity in Havana, Miranda had been assigned the task of escorting this distinguished prisoner around town, a duty that the aide-de-camp enjoyed since it gave him the opportunity to practice his English. Unfortunately, General Campbell was mistakenly permitted to visit the Spanish forts guarding the harbor. Military sites such as these were off limits to anyone who might report their condition to the enemy. Although Miranda was not responsible for this slip in vigilance, not even being present when it happened, many blamed him for the error since he was often in the general's company. The Gálvez family decided that Cagigal's assistant was an incorrigible Anglophile who could not be trusted.[9]

As a result of all these difficulties José de Gálvez, the minister of the Indies, issued an order for Miranda to be apprehended and sent back to Spain. In fact, he issued several arrest orders. Cagigal, however, managed to fend off their enforcement by keeping Miranda at his side. The captain general was Miranda's shield, tenuous as it was, against incarceration. Yet Cagigal also misinterpreted how serious the case against Miranda was. He seemed to feel that the glory of military success would sweep past peccadilloes away. By sending Miranda to the Cape, Cagigal placed his aide-de-camp outside his direct protection and in the hands of Bernardo de Gálvez, nephew of the minister of the Indies. At a moment when Miranda expected the adulation and congratulations of his fellow military officers at the Cape, he found himself instead placed under arrest. Bernardo de Gálvez sent him back to Havana for deportation to Spain. The news that he had brought to the Cape about Nassau seemed to have made no difference at all in his personal fortune or that of his superior, Cagigal.

Astute enough to realize the gravity of his personal situation, Miranda still could not restrain himself from lashing out at his immediate tormentors, the Gálvez family. He wrote and published in the French newspaper at the Cape a glowing and laudatory description of the conquest of New Providence, omitting the estrangement between Gillon and Cagigal and also leaving out a politically necessary bow to the superior who had permitted the expedition in the first place, namely Bernardo de Gálvez.[10] He sent off a similar version to be printed in the American newspapers, an account which barely mentioned that Gillon had tagged along.[11]

The embattled aide did not neglect to report his woes to Cagigal, who was told that the entire Gálvez family was consumed with jealousy at the captain general's success and that the newspaper story of the victory at New Providence had provoked tears of anger and envy from Bernardo. According to Miranda, the Spanish general lamented bitterly that French newspapers never praised him and his family in a similar vein. So hostile had Gálvez become that Miranda blamed him for rumors at the Cape that the captain general had made 500,000 pesos from the New Providence expedition.[12] What Miranda had done, in effect, was to poison the environment between the governor of Cuba and his commanding officer. A friendly Bernardo de Gálvez could not have saved Miranda at this point, but he could have prevented some of the conflict with the Spanish navy which faced Cagigal.

While Miranda chafed at his unexpected confinement at the Cape, his commander faced a new problem growing out of Gillon's decision to forsake the Spanish forces in the Bahamas. When Cagigal forwarded the news about the surrender of Nassau to Havana, he did not mention his rupture with the commodore. Others in the Bahamas, however, did. Realizing that the Spanish army had almost no naval protection to convoy the transports home nor any naval personnel to direct the fleet, Juan Dabán, interim governor in Cagigal's absence, called an emergency meeting of the war council in Havana on 25 May 1782. This council decided to ask the chief naval commander in the port to detach some Spanish frigates to cover the returning transports.[13] This was done immediately. But in Cagigal's haste to reach Havana quickly he decided to allow the victorious expedition to proceed home in two groups —the first being a small number of ships that arrived with Cagigal in Havana on June 1 and the second a much larger squadron that mostly made its way back under Brigadier General Mannrique. Since the Spanish frigates did not know the number of ships arriving, the date to expect them, or the return route, they could hardly provide much protection.

In fact, the frigates failed to sight either of the two homeward-bound convoys. The first group, with Cagigal, made it safely to Havana, luckily missing an English fleet that blockaded Havana for a few days just after this Spanish flotilla made port. The second group, under Mannrique, had a different experience. This squadron hit extremely foul weather in the Bahama Channel, which scattered many of the ships. Some headed for Havana, others scurried back to Nassau, and the bulk rendezvoused off Bimini and waited for nature to turn a fair face.

After realizing that they had exhausted their supplies waiting for good sailing weather, leaders of the Bimini group tried to return to Nassau for stores. British privateers attacked these ships and dispersed them. Although the privateers were eventually driven off, a few of the Spanish ships made for Havana and spread the word that part of the convoy had fallen into enemy hands. The truth was that several had been lost momentarily but had been quickly retaken. The entire convoy eventually reached Havana, but the disorganized manner of its arrival and the many reports of disaster beclouded a victorious homecoming.[14] Indeed, the whole episode raised the serious and inevitable question of why the Spanish navy had not participated in the expedition in the first place.

Since animosities already existed between the Spanish army and navy, Admiral Solano, who was at the Cape during most of the New Providence campaign, realized that a catastrophe involving the returning fleet might be blamed on the navy for not providing an escort. Protecting his political flank, the admiral promptly wrote to his ministry in Madrid that he had never been consulted or asked to participate in the New Providence campaign. As a result the navy, Solano maintained, could certainly not be faulted for any loses among the homeward-bound troop convoys. Solano's letter caused the expected result in Spain. The minister of marine demanded an explanation from the army for the absence of Spanish naval participation in this affair.

When Bernardo de Gálvez, the principal Spanish commander in the Caribbean, was queried about this, he placed all the blame on Cagigal. With no love for Solano and with the memory of Miranda's visit fresh in his mind, Gálvez replied that he had no idea why the captain general had used foreign rather than Spanish ships for escorts. This was, of course, an incredible lapse of memory. Gálvez finished his response by recalling that Cagigal had once said to him that no expedition would ever get ashore if it depended upon the Spanish navy for help.

Working together efficiently for perhaps the only time in their careers, Solano and Gálvez effectively conspired to bring down upon the head of Cagigal the full wrath of a sensitive and outraged Spanish navy.[15] Under normal circumstances Cagigal would have had the support of his fellow army officers and his immediate superiors. In this case, however, Bernardo de Gálvez and the Gálvez family were happy to let Cagigal defend himself, if he could. It cost the hard-pressed general a great deal of money and ten years of time to clear his name of these and other charges. Moreover, during this decade Cagigal was either imprisoned or under house arrest. Not until the French invaded Spain in 1793 would Cagigal again lead Spanish soldiers.[16]

The New Providence campaign ended on an unhappy note for many of the principal participants on the victorious side. Even Miranda, certainly no revolutionary at this point in his life, fully understood that his Spanish military career was disintegrating and that he was still free only because of Cagigal's personal power. By the end of 1782 Cagigal would no longer command in Havana and had orders to return to Spain to face the charges against him. As a result, Miranda fled Havana early in 1783 for the United States. There, ironically enough, his New Providence past momentarily caught up with him. Traveling through Charleston in 1783, Miranda encountered some people who had sailed on the *South Carolina* and who remembered the Spanish translator well. One of them, William Brailsford, a member of a prominent merchant family in the city, challenged the former aide-de-camp to a duel, alleging that Miranda had mistreated Americans at Nassau. The duel never took place because Miranda convinced his challenger that others, principally Cagigal, had been responsible for the troubles that upset Brailsford.[17] Nevertheless, Miranda was hardly a heroic figure in the eyes of many Americans on that expedition.

Chapter Four

NUEVA PROVIDENCIA

The Bahamas remained Spanish for a little more than eleven months—8 May 1782 to 19 April 1783. During this period the newly acquired colony had two, three, or four Spanish governors, depending upon whether one counts General Cagigal as the first governor, he remained only two weeks in Nassau and never referred to himself as governor, and depending upon how one handles Cagigal's successor, Captain Antonio Claraco y Sanz, who served in the post twice. The chronology of the principal Spanish officials in the Bahamas was:

General Juan Manuel de Cagigal (8 May 1782 to 24 May 1782),

Captain Antonio Claraco y Sanz (24? May 1782 to 18 September 1782),

Captain Raymundo Andrés (18 September 1782 to 14 January 1783), and

Captain Antonio Claraco y Sanz (15 January 1783 to 19 April 1783).[1]

The frequent rotation of leaders at the top indicates how troubled Spanish rule in Nassau was. The Spaniards found it far easier to conquer than to govern New Providence.

The most pressing problem at the beginning of the Spanish occupation of the Bahamas was facilitating the return of the expeditionary forces that had conquered Nassau and organizing a Spanish government and garrison. Sending the expedition back to Havana went badly. The last soldier and sailor slated to sail home did not

42

depart from Nassau until early July 1782 which was far behind
the schedule approved by Bernardo de Gálvez. The burden of
feeding so many unexpected troops and finding proper escorts
for each of the two convoy groups fell upon Nassau, stripping
the port of many ships and supplies. A considerable amount of
war booty, particularly weapons and materials taken from corsairs,
also found its way to Cuba at this time.[2] What was left behind
after early July in Nassau was a modest Spanish garrison of some
300 soldiers and a tiny naval force of 7 small ships manned by
nearly 150 sailors. Eventually this military component would be
joined by a small Spanish merchant community and a number of
Americans. Although in total numbers this was a minor Spanish
outpost, the size of the Spanish military presence in Nassau was
very impressive compared to the minuscule English garrisons of
earlier days. With a total British population of 2,750 individuals
on New Providence in 1782, the 450 soldiers and sailors, plus as-
sorted foreigners and Spanish civilians, composed a sizeable portion of the island's inhabitants.[3]

The Spanish garrison was also the Spanish government for the
Bahamas, a situation which created one of the most serious problems facing the recently arrived administrators of New Providence.
Since the conquering army had come essentially from Havana, and
since it was a military exercise that operated in the shadow of the
combined Franco-Hispanic army in St. Domingue preparing to attack Jamaica, General Cagigal had a relatively free hand picking
officials to rule New Providence. Cagigal naturally selected military
officers who were loyal to himself. These men were trusted, came
from similar backgrounds as his, and could be expected to defend
the island if the British attempted to take it back. Antonio Claraco
y Sanz, Cagigal's choice to command the garrison and govern the
colony, was a perfect example of the captain general's appointees.

Claraco had come to Havana in the same fleet that had brought
Cagigal and Miranda from Spain (the Solano convoy of 1780). He
was Aragonese, as was evidently Raymundo de Andrés, the next
Spanish governor of the Bahamas; and it was quite possible that
Miranda, an officer in the Regiment of Aragon, played a role in
Claraco's selection. Although a young man Claraco was a seasoned
veteran, having participated in the capture of Santa Catalina from
the Portuguese in 1777.[4] Within the general scheme of Spanish
patronage the new governor was part of the Cagigal entourage,
dependent upon the captain general for professional advance-

ment. Claraco was in the same position regarding Cagigal as the captain general was to Bernardo de Gálvez, commander of the expeditionary army at Cape François. The advantages of such a patronage system were very obvious, but the disadvantages were also apparent. Cagigal's political enemies became those of Claraco —and Cagigal had numerous adversaries who would not hesitate to make the life of a protégé of the captain general miserable.

Nothing, thus, could or did stop the factionalism of Cuban politics from spreading immediately to the Bahamas. The one branch of Spanish government that neither Cagigal nor Claraco controlled in the Bahamas was that of the royal exchequer. Since responsibility for financial and civilian matters in Cuba was split between Intendant Urriza and Captain General Cagigal, authority for these two functions was also separated in Nassau. Intendant Urriza had assigned exchequer officials to accompany Cagigal's expedition to the Bahamas. Indeed, these very officials had much to do with Havana receiving the earliest reports of the dissension between the captain general and Commodore Gillon. Most of these treasury officials then remained in the Bahamas to operate the exchequer during the occupation.[5] All the animosities that existed between Cagigal and Urriza in Havana soon manifested themselves in the relations between Claraco and his colleagues in the treasury.

Only a little spark was needed to set off these altercations. Such a spark came easily in the numerous areas where lines of authority overlapped. Treasury officials challenged Claraco's right to permit incoming ships to land and sell their cargoes. Since there were good reasons to send out many truce ships to nearby British colonies, these same officials accused the governor of using such vessels as a means to smuggle illegal merchandise into the Bahamas—the very same accusation that Urriza employed so effectively against Cagigal in Havana. The Bahamian exchequer decided that most incoming goods for Nassau were foreign in origin and hence subject to the highest import taxes—double what was being collected in Havana on the very same products. These high levies threatened to drive away many American merchants whose trade was necessary if New Providence was to receive food supplies. An exasperated Claraco, young and very inexperienced in such bureaucratic squabbles, fired off a number of letters to Cagigal and Urriza complaining about the exchequer on the island. Evidently the governor even succumbed to challenging his bureaucratic adversaries to meet on the field of honor, hardly the way to handle office politics.

Claraco maintained that by spending so much time on financial matters he was forced to divert attention from the defense of the island against a possible British strike.[6] Although the Spanish governor certainly had a sympathetic ear in the person of the captain general in Havana, by the summer of 1782 power had shifted so much in Cuba in favor of the intendancy that Cagigal decided to remove Claraco temporarily in August to pacify treasury complaints.[7] Captain Raymundo Andrés took Claraco's place and was able to keep internecine squabbling with the treasury under control. Unlike Claraco, Andrés developed a healthy respect for the power of the accountant's pen. Just before Cagigal was relieved of his command in Havana at the end of 1782, knowing that he had lost his struggle with Urriza, the captain general sent Claraco back to the island in one last act of defiance against his domestic enemies. Although the dispute no longer flourished as it once had, exchequer officials never forgot it.

While the top Spanish officials in the Bahamas bickered among themselves, the entire occupying force had to deal with the complex undertaking of governing the local population of the Bahamas. There was the mundane but critical problem of language. The conquerors spoke one tongue, native residents another. Unlike the inhabitants of other British Caribbean islands close to Spanish territory, few Bahamians spoke or read Spanish, an indication of the colony's trade patterns. Once most of the Spanish expeditionary force left Nassau, the new governors constantly requested literate translators from Havana. Eventually this need was partially met by an Irish Catholic priest, Father Miguel O'Reilly, who was sent to fulfill linguistic as well as spiritual functions for the government and garrison. Yet the problem of translators was never adequately solved because there were certain duties that O'Reilly felt were inappropriate for a man of the cloth.[8] Clerics should not, he thought, involve themselves as translators in legal disputes, precisely where there was a demand for people who understood both tongues.

While language was one problem, there was also the matter of rewarding people who had helped the expedition. A small but significant group of Bahamian residents had actively collaborated in the success of the Hispano-American assault. A few of these may have been Americans who lived on New Providence.[9] Yet whether they were outsiders or locals, those who stayed in Nassau after May 1782 expected and received special consideration from the

Spanish government. Some obtained trading privileges with Cuba. Others received income-producing positions in the colony's capital.[10] Although these active collaborators constituted only a small faction, the rest of the population was not overtly hostile to the Spanish occupation. Certainly at the beginning of the new rule most Bahamians cooperated with their new masters passively, and some far more than that. Indeed, the question of Bahamian loyalty to England throughout the war was an open one.

Since the capitulation agreement mandated that the islands were to remain under English law and custom, the Spanish government kept most local officials in their offices, imposing Spanish supervision only at the very top. Even the highest Bahamian officials, especially members of the colony's council, continued to perform some of their usual functions. It was quite common for a councilor to sit also as a judge or magistrate.[11] The Out Islands retained their own officials and hardly saw a Spaniard unless one of their citizens visited the capital.[12] The British courts in Nassau remained open, wills were proved, and marriages performed. Even the clerical staff and chief secretary to the British governor remained in their positions.

Those who felt that they had been abused by the dominant faction in the pre-Spanish milieu now had an opportunity to get some measure of revenge through leverage with the Spaniards. William Bradford, secretary to the islands' governor and a strong supporter of ex-Governor Montfort Browne, was perhaps the best example of this. He became the most important English official during the Spanish occupation. Nearly all important Spanish decrees were countersigned by Bradford in his capacity as secretary to the governor. Although what Bradford did was little different from the actions of other local public officials, he would be singled out for punishment after the war.[13] Again, this had more to do with pre-Spanish politics in New Providence than it did with collaboration.

Most members of the mercantile community, even John Miller, later famous for his opposition to the Spaniards, made their peace early with the new conquerors. Such a large garrison as the Spanish proposed to leave in Nassau would need a lot of supplies, and there was no reason why local entrepreneurs should not furnish these goods. Many did. Certainly Miller and others showed little initial reluctance to trade with their country's enemies.[14] If the Spaniards opened Nassau as widely to trade as they had Havana, the entire business community stood to benefit during an otherwise trying time. Just as it had been the wealthier Bahamians who pressured Maxwell not to resist the invasion, it was this group that also restrained the few early cases of open opposition to Spanish rule.

When the first Spanish ships left Nassau to return to Havana, bonfires lit the coastline of New Providence to mark their departure. As was learned later, local sailors ashore set these fires to warn English corsairs that ships were leaving. The purpose of the signals may have been to alert nearby privateers so they could attack stragglers. The intention could also have been to warn British ships to scatter. The Spaniards suspected the former. Local officials informed the conquerors about the nature of the groups who had set these signals, and the garrison sent patrols to prevent a recurrence of such warnings when the next ships departed.

Yet it was with the very next departures that resistance of another sort emerged. The large convoy under Brigadier General Mannrique needed Bahamian pilots to lead it through the dangerous waters in the island chain. Those pilots who had accompanied the original expedition had evidently left with Cagigal and were not available. The remaining pilots in Nassau refused to cooperate. Some hid in the town, others refused to exercise their skills for the new conquerors. Leaders of the Bahamian government interceded on behalf of the hard-pressed Spaniards by hunting down the fugitives and delivering them, bound when necessary, to Spanish officials. They also used their persuasive powers to convince those who had not gone into hiding but who were still reluctant to help to change their minds.[15] If the humbler elements of Bahamian society found it distasteful to work for the enemy, the powerful and wealthy initially did not. During the first weeks and months conqueror and conquered enjoyed a honeymoon. It did not last.

By late June local attitudes toward the Spaniards began to change, at least those attitudes expressed by an influential segment of the merchant class in Nassau. There were a number of reasons for this, some quite general in nature, others growing out of specific incidents. Of those general in scope the economic prosperity of New Providence was the most critical. The Bahamas had thrived in the years just prior to the conquest partly because the war against the American rebels on the mainland had shifted to the southern colonies, placing Nassau in an ideal location to trade with the most active of the remaining British armies. By 1782 British fortunes were on the decline on the continent, and the Spanish government in Nassau permitted no trade with colonies under enemy control. Consequently the commerce of New Providence dropped dramatically after the Spanish arrival. Spanish friends such as the Americans, although extremely important, could not make up this deficit, and neutral shipping was not permitted.

The jurisdictional contest between Governor Claraco and the exchequer also adversely affected the few American ships and cargoes that did arrive. Many Americans felt there was little incentive to call at Nassau when ships there had to wait for the Spanish bureaucracy to settle its disputes before unloading their goods. Far more lucrative markets at Havana and the Cape offered fewer difficulties. Hence, except for a few that combined a stop at Nassau with a voyage to or from Havana, American ships avoided Nassau. Even expansion of the modest Spanish merchant community provided few trading opportunities for resident entrepreneurs. The number of ships to and from Havana dwindled substantially the longer the Spaniards stayed in the Bahamas.[16] Foreign occupation of the British colony thus ushered in a period of very restricted trade and economic depression.

Commercial hard times, however, were not the principal factor in turning local merchants against the Spaniards. Bad as Nassau might be for the moment, it certainly was a safer place than Charleston or St. Augustine, the two closest British ports still in friendly hands. The biggest source of income for Nassau during the American Revolution had been the war itself. Privateering had been particularly prosperous. The longer the war had lasted, the more lucrative privateering had become.[17] It would be grossly unfair to describe the typical Bahamian trader as a "merchant of death," but a substantial part of the colony's income was generated from arming and manning corsairs, followed by condemnation and sale of captured spoils. Investors in Nassau had fitted out as many as twelve large privateers in the 14- to 20-gun range, not to mention dozens of lesser vessels engaged in the same activity. Spanish court records show an astounding amount of war goods in the possession of certain Nassau merchants. If some armies were strapped for military supplies during these war years, the corsair merchants of Nassau were not.

The Spaniards, of course, were generally aware of what had been happening throughout New Providence. Indeed, privateering had made the Bahamas a prime target for Spanish retaliation once the war with Great Britain had begun. Yet the new conquerors were not prepared for the extent and scope of corsair activities which existed in the islands. Captured documents in Nassau showed the Spaniards that in the four and a half years before May 1782 the Bahamian admiralty court had condemned 172 ships brought in by privateers. The overwhelming majority of these ships were American (124), but there was also a sizable minority of Spanish (15) and French (31) vessels.[18] The Spanish ships taken into Nassau generally carried cargo worth much more than that of the American and French vessels, and the Spanish losses had increased substantially just before the invasion of 1782.[19]

Although privateering was an established institution with accepted international rules in the eighteenth century, corsairs were not particularly admired people. In an era when most long distance travel was done by sailing ship, privateers made sea travel even more risky. Moreover, corsairs occupied a judicial gray area in which they were not members of the enemy's military and therefore not eligible for rights granted prisoners of war, yet neither were they innocent civilians whose treatment fell under another set of conventions. In the surrender agreement negotiated by Governor Maxwell corsairs and their owners were subject only to the loss of their military goods (cannons, muskets, gunpowder, and other materials of war). This was a substantial loss for some merchants. Alexander Roxbourgh, for example, had nearly $4,500 worth of military stores seized by the Spanish after the British surrender, among which were 20 cannons (12 pounders).[20] John Miller, another entrepreneur, lost $14,500 worth of armaments, including 90 cannons of various sizes, 185 muskets, and 2,550 pounds of gunpowder.[21] These financial setbacks, however, were not as significant as the losses that many Bahamians might have suffered had the Spaniards fought and subdued the colony by force. Then they would have imposed their own terms of surrender. What made the corsair owners understandably nervous about their past activities was the knowledge that the Spaniards believed that some of the residents of Nassau continued their privateering ventures.

When New Providence fell to the Spaniards, they were pleased by the number of corsair ships trapped in the harbor of Nassau. Had the sailors who manned those vessels been involved in the defense of Nassau, the numerical advantage held by the Spaniards would have been much less. Not all Bahamian corsairs, however, were in port when the invaders struck. It was those still at sea that soon presented problems for the conquerors and for their sponsors.

A few days after the capture of New Providence, Governor Claraco ordered that all ship owners turn in a list of their absent vessels.[22] Claraco then gave the owners two months to bring their ships into port. He also gave Nassau merchants permission to search for their ships at sea. Those that came in within the stipulated time were to be treated like those already in Nassau when it fell to Cagigal. The Spaniards proposed to register the vessels and return them to their masters. If these vessels had been corsairs, they would be stripped of their weapons before being released. Those not meeting the deadline were to be treated as prizes whenever they fell into Spanish hands. Two months was a very generous time limit since most Bahamian privateers sailed close to home and undoubtedly were aware of the proclamation within a short time. Yet there were obviously some strong incentives not to obey this Spanish decree.

Cautious corsairs at sea waited to see how the Spaniards treated the population of New Providence. Rumors in some nearby British colonies suggested that the entire population of Nassau had fled into the interior to escape the jurisdiction of the conquerors. Since the Spaniards were definitely going to confiscate corsair weapons, it made good business sense to dock first in a British port, sell these armaments, and then return to Nassau.[23] Some of the corsairs also carried booty of their own.[24] Since Spanish losses had grown during the early months of 1782, Spanish victims had almost certainly contributed to this corsair loot. Common sense dictated that these goods be sold or deposited in a safe location rather than risking them to an unknown fate in Nassau. There was only one case of a privateer voluntarily coming into port after the Spanish invasion.[25] Numerous records do exist, however, of Bahamian privateers continuing their trade in close proximity to home. The first instance of this was a very critical one.

While returning to Havana, the principal Spanish troop convoy was attacked by two corsairs on 11 June near Bimini. The Bahamian pilots on board the lead ships, who in several cases were reluctant crew members, recognized the privateers. In sworn statements several of the pilots later identified one of the corsairs as either the Nassau privateer *The Enterprise* or a ship very similar in appearance. Other Bahamians with the fleet thought that they saw a local corsair called *The Unicorn* with the privateers.[26] The owners of these two ships still resided in New Providence. The commander of the Spanish fleet, Brigadier General José Mannrique, was forced to return to Nassau, in part because of these corsairs. Furious at the unexpected assault, he ordered Governor Claraco to arrest the disloyal owners of these ships, people Mannrique referred to as *estos infidentes*.[27] In his mind they had clearly broken the capitulation agreements signed only a month or so earlier.

When word reached Havana about corsair activity against the returning convoy, General Cagigal also ordered the governor to take immediate action against the *armadores* of these privateers. Cagigal was as upset by this attack as was Mannrique. He had been informed initially that one of his own ships, the *San Antonio de Menchaca*, had been lost, information that was only partially correct because the corsairs failed to hold the ships they took. The captain general was also disturbed because the apparent success of the corsair attack gave substance to his critics who faulted Cagigal for relying on foreigners like Gillon to protect his fleet.

Matters rapidly deteriorated for those merchants in Nassau who could be connected to these privateers or to any of the others still away when evidence started to surface that many corsair captains did not present themselves in port after hearing about the Spanish conquest of the Bahamas. The Spaniards further learned that some captains had been in contact with their owners in Nassau after the fall of New Providence. Several corsairs had even landed on a deserted stretch of the island's coast sailors who wished to be with their families in New Providence.[28] At almost the same time that the convoy was under attack, another Bahamian corsair, *The Fox*, had sailed for Bermuda to sell her cannons in anticipation of returning home. On the way *The Fox* evidently captured two ships, one American and the other French. The latter's crew and passengers were sent to Nassau, where the French captain protested vigorously that the seizure of his ship was illegal. He felt that the owners of *The Fox* were bound by the capitulation accord to stop preying on enemy shipping since they lived in New Providence.[29] Bahamian merchants were nervous about how the Spaniards would react to these events, and they did not have to wait long to witness the consequences.

Ownership of *The Enterprise*, *The Unicorn*, and *The Fox* was not hard to determine. The new government already had a list of ships still at sea. If that list were not complete, there were plenty of people in Nassau eager, for one reason or another, to clarify the question of the guilty *armadores*. The English pilots with the convoy reported that *The Enterprise* was owned by Thomas Roker, Nicholas Garner, Robert Hunt, and one other unidentified person. Officials ashore traced *The Unicorn* to John Miller and *The Fox* to Alexander Roxbourgh. Other residents—either captains of privateers, like Joseph Hunter and Daniel Wheeler, or owners of additional corsairs operating in the Bahamian waters, like John Ferguson—were brought to the attention of Spanish authorities.[30] The government eventually took action in one form or another against seventeen individuals, actually arresting or seizing property from fourteen. This was only a small percentage of the population of New Providence, but many of these residents were people of considerable resources and with political connections to defend themselves.[31] Those with the most Bahamian property and those who were physically present in Nassau faced the greatest danger since they were the most vulnerable to direct punishment. It was this group that made up the fourteen who felt the sting of Spanish justice, and it was this group that complained the most.

Spanish retaliation against the corsair merchants of New Providence came in two flurries of activity—the first directed by Governor Claraco in July and August 1782 and the second beginning a month later under the new interim governor, Raymundo Andrés. In the first period Governor Claraco ordered the arrest of those known to be connected with the corsairs *Enterprise, Unicorn,* and *Fox.* Those apprehended faced various punishments. John Miller, for example, was confined to Claraco's house for a while, then detained in Fort Nassau (the largest military base in the capital), and finally restricted to house arrest. Others were evidently held for the entire period at Fort Nassau. In order to be released from the strictest confinement, those charged with abetting privateers had to post bond against the potential damages done by their ships at sea. The governor next seized business property belonging to the accused, had it inventoried, and then decreed that all who owed debts to the corsair merchants had to turn in such funds to authorities within three days. Failure to comply with the deadline resulted in fines four times as large as the amount owed. Governor Claraco encouraged informants to denounce those ignoring the proclamation by offering a reward of one hundred dollars for information on possible delinquents and promising to keep names of cooperating individuals secret.[32]

In the transient and divided merchant community of Nassau these measures succeeded in prying loose substantial amounts of money for the Spaniards. In some cases there were innocent victims. Some merchants whose business transactions intertwined with those of the accused found their funds confiscated by the Spaniards.[33] These rather draconic measures, however, did not stop corsair activity around the Bahamas.

Those affected by the Spanish measures certainly did not accept their fate passively. They protested to Spanish officials in Havana that they could not be held responsible for ships at sea whose locations they did not know. They also pleaded for assistance from nearby British colonies and business acquaintances, asking that British authorities threaten similar actions against Spanish citizens.[34] How effective these efforts were is not clear. In fact, they may well have been counterproductive. Yet they most certainly played a role in the next series of actions against the *armadores*.

In September 1782 Captain General Cagigal decided to remove Governor Claraco temporarily from his post in Nassau. This decision was prompted by the bitter struggle for power between the treasury and military authorities in New Providence, a reflection of the same dispute in Cuba. Punishment dealt out to the *armadores* was also a factor in Claraco's recall. Cagigal believed that the governor had been too lenient on the most notorious of those involved in the Bahamian privateering, principally John Miller, Thomas Roker, and Alexander Roxbourgh. The new interim governor, Raymundo Andrés, carried with him strict instructions concerning the treatment of these merchants.[35] If Andrés needed an additional incentive to be zealous in complying with the captain general's orders, he found it on the way to New Providence when his ship was chased into the harbor at Nassau by a corsair.[36]

Cagigal had ordered Andrés to rearrest Miller, Roker, and Roxbourgh immediately. This Andrés did as soon as he landed. Unlike Claraco, who had eventually allowed the three to serve a gentlemen's confinement under house arrest, Andrés sent them all to Fort Nassau. Following his instructions, the new governor gave the merchants a choice between being transported to Havana to stand trial for violating the surrender capitulations or posting a bond of 300,000 pesos with the Havana treasury while the charges were considered by a Cuban court. If they chose the latter alternative, they were required to ship the money to Cuba at their own expense and peril—ironically running the risk of capture by corsairs. All three claimed that they could not produce such funds, and they would not anyway even if they could.[37] Consequently Andrés sent them off to Havana at the end of October, along with four other Bahamians—Captain Joseph Hunter, his lieutenant Ralph Moulton, and two others from Miller's corsair, the *Unicorn*, who had unwisely come to Nassau by small boat to visit their families.[38] They had expected the Spaniards to leave them alone, even though they had not brought in Miller's corsair to be disarmed.

Once they were in Havana, Cagigal had Miranda escort the seven to the Morro fortress and prison, where they all remained until the war was over. Like most prisons of the day the Morro provided different levels of treatment and accommodation for its guests. For those who could afford it, the Spanish prison offered adequate lodging and food. For those who could not, the Morro prison was a miserable place which barely provided the necessities to keep prisoners alive. The Bahamian merchants fared reasonably well in these circumstances. They even had their own menservants in attendance. The other islanders fared less well, although Miller made certain that his corsair captain, Hunter, had enough funds to sustain himself.[39] All the prisoners went on trial after the war, and the outcome of this judicial proceeding proved to be important in the affairs of New Providence.

The difficulties experienced by the New Providence *armadores* produced an unexpected, but very welcomed, benefit for the Spaniards. Because of the heavy wartime demands upon the Cuban treasury to support a large garrison in Havana, the Spanish navy in the New World, a large expeditionary force poised in Cape François, and an impoverished French navy and army in the Caribbean, Intendant Urriza had few, if any, funds to shuttle north to New Providence.[40] Governor Claraco in Nassau estimated that his monthly expenses were about 5,000 pesos. The financial records for the Spanish garrison in the Bahamas showed a slightly higher monthly average than the governor's calculations. Except for the modest funds that arrived with the conquering expedition in May 1782, no other currency shipment arrived from Havana during the war.[41] As a result the government in the Bahamas had to finance itself. This was hardly a unique situation since many Spanish posts in the Caribbean did the same. In New Providence, however, government financing was handled in a singular way. Slightly more than 60 percent of the income of the Nassau exchequer during the Spanish occupation (nearly 200,000 pesos) came from confiscated property, cash, and debts owed the *armadores*. Personal loans from Spanish merchants and army officers in New Providence (73,000 pesos, constituting 21 percent of the total income) made up the next major source of revenue for the exchequer.[42]

To some extent Spanish financing was a modified version of an army living off the land. The biggest handicap to such a system of raising money, all most carefully recorded and itemized in the New Providence treasury records, was that the accused merchants were ultimately subject to a Spanish judicial hearing of their case in Havana. The Spanish legal system provided justice for those who could afford it, and the *armadores* from Nassau could. The bond of 300,000 pesos—Cagigal's alternative to imprisonment for Miller, Roker, and Roxbourgh—had not been a wildly exaggerated guess at what these merchants could afford. Should the Bahamians be able to clear themselves of violating the capitulation accords, the Spanish government would be obligated to repay these funds.

While understandable from an emotional and financial perspective, the Spanish retribution against the New Providence merchants cost the new conquerors dearly. This chastisement changed the psychological temper of the occupation. The arrests and seizures directly affected only a handful of Bahamian citizens, and perhaps twenty more felt the sting of losing money owed in debts to the *armadores*. Yet who in New Providence was safe? It was possible for the Spaniards to link privateering to many more people in the colony, and there was considerable confusion as to where Spanish revenge would end. What seemed to Spaniards to be careful and appropriate punishment meted out to rogues hiding behind masks of mercantile respectability appeared to many islanders to be capricious and threatening conduct. From a population that had passively accepted the conquest and had been willing to make the best of an uncertain situation, many Bahamians, particularly men of property and merchants, now wanted to leave, if they could. The capitulation accords signed by Cagigal and Maxwell permitted this.[43] But many could not easily depart, and they constituted a segment of the Bahamian populace ripe for action against the conquerors.

Chapter Five

FALL OF THE
SPANISH BAHAMAS

Unlike the British, the Spaniards were serious about defending New Providence. Spanish intention to do so was reflected in the size and quality of the garrison which Cagigal left behind in the summer of 1782. To protect Nassau the captain general detailed nearly three hundred soldiers and officers from two line regiments—that of España and that of Corona of Mexico. The España troops had seen action at Pensacola and were considered first-rate soldiers.[1] The Corona regiment did not have quite as good a reputation, stigmatized in the eyes of many regular officers for being American staffed and led;[2] yet it was more experienced than the militia and invalids which Governor Maxwell had relied on earlier. A small detachment of artillerymen also served with the garrison. In addition, Cagigal assigned a small flotilla of seven launches and brigantines manned by 157 sailors to the defenses of Nassau.[3] Close to shore or in the narrow confines of the harbor these boats were a naval force to be reckoned with since they had considerable maneuverability and carried heavy cannon. Given time to improve the modest British military works, most Spanish officers thought that their garrison could resist an invading force of two thousand soldiers long enough for help to arrive from Havana.[4] Antonio Claraco y Sanz and Raymundo Andrés, commanding officers of this Spanish force, were soldiers who had demonstrated considerable courage in their military careers. Some of their other abilities, however, were open to question.

56

At several points in the nearly twelve months of Spanish rule, it appeared that the Bahamas might be attacked. The first threat occurred within weeks of the capture of New Providence when the British frigate *HMS Garland* was sighted near the port of Nassau. Like the *South Carolina* the *Garland* was big enough to dominate the waters of the Bahama chain. The *Garland*'s captain probably knew that New Providence had fallen to the Spaniards since his ship failed to pursue a fleeing Spanish ship into Nassau's harbor. At any rate the *Garland* anchored east of Nassau and sent an exploratory party ashore. Claraco, correctly guessing where this party might land, ambushed and apprehended the entire British detachment with its landing boat. Then the governor organized an early morning assault on the frigate itself. Catching the British man-of-war unprepared for such a challenge, Claraco and his unorthodox naval flotilla panicked the frigate's crew and officers, forcing the *Garland* to beat a hasty retreat, abandoning several anchors and cables in the process.[5]

While the *Garland* had been a solitary harassment, the next danger seemed far more ominous. On 1 July 1782 the early morning watch reported a large convoy of English ships preparing to enter the harbor. Having heard rumors from civilian informers of an impending British invasion led by two frigates and a ship of the line (*navio*), Claraco prepared frantically to defend the islands. His first fear was that the general population of the island might rise. Despite the postconquest disarmament of the Nassau citizenry, the governor felt that the number of weapons confiscated had been paltry. He did not trust the neutrality of the Bahamians during a British attack. Consequently Claraco summoned the remaining leaders of the Maxwell government and threatened to fire on the residents of the city if they did not evacuate the town immediately. They were to leave behind only enough people to assist the Spaniards with the wounded at the hospital. The city fathers promised to do just that.

Claraco next turned his attention to the growing number of ships off shore. In spite of the fact that the watch reported that these vessels were flying Spanish colors, the convoy was clearly English from the design of the foremost ships, all obviously British built. It was a common ruse to display enemy standards to gain time for deployment. Before the shore batteries could obey Claraco's orders to fire on the closest vessels, the convoy's flagship sent a skiff ashore. Claraco learned to his relief and embarrassment that

his visitors were indeed Spanish. In fact, this convoy was the very
one that had left the Bahamas two weeks earlier for Havana, only
to become becalmed off the Biminis and then chased back to Nassau by Bahamian corsairs.[6] Claraco's repressive treatment of
Nassau's residents during this false alarm would not be forgotten
by many people. On the other hand, the governor's instinctive distrust of the local population's loyalty and his fear that a hostile
citizenry would pose a potential threat to the security of the garrison proved to be only too accurate later on.

Confident that the garrison would have acquitted itself well had
any of these threats to Spanish rule been realized, Governors Claraco and Andrés busied themselves with improving the old British
fortifications. Claraco established a daily schedule whereby one-
fourth of his soldiers were on guard, one-half resting, and one-
fourth working on new defenses.[7] The two main military struc-
tures in New Providence were Fort Montague, a modest enclosure
about three miles east of town which defended the eastern sea
approach to the harbor, and Fort Nassau, a more imposing edifice
in the middle of town designed to protect the western sea entrance
to the harbor. Both of these forts had serious defects, the worst
of which was that neither was constructed to withstand a serious
land assault. Against ships both sites were formidable; against a
land force they both could be taken easily. Claraco, whose military
specialty was fortifications, worked to improve both and to build
new strong points to remedy the problem of dealing with an enemy
army. The most important Spanish addition to the defense of New
Providence was a citadel—called the *Casa Fuerte*—surrounding
the governor's house.[8] This structure was located in the hills overlooking the harbor and Fort Nassau. It would be very difficult
to take by direct assault and could be a last refuge during a long
siege.

With the passage of time the British threat to the Bahamas increased substantially. Ironically, it was British failure elsewhere
that accounted for this. The defeat at Yorktown in 1781 left British
forces in the southern colonies confined to the three coastal towns
of Wilmington, Charleston, and Savannah. Increasingly British authorities in these three cities saw their control over the hinterlands
deteriorate. By the winter of 1782 the British government had
abandoned all three sites. Charleston, by far the most important
southern city in British hands, saw the last Union Jack pulled down
in mid-December. The greater part of retreating British troops,

loyalist militia, and other faithful subjects headed south to East Florida, the closest British possession. Inundated with soldiers, transports, naval vessels, and uprooted loyalists, St. Augustine (East Florida's capital) was only a few days sailing distance from Nassau. From December 1782 onward the Spanish governors in Nassau received constant warnings that they were about to be attacked by the British from East Florida.

Spanish intelligence from St. Augustine was remarkably accurate about what was transpiring in the capital of East Florida. Using spies as well as friendly Bahamians who maintained frequent contacts with Florida, Governor Claraco kept abreast of the ships moving in and out of St. Augustine (including the arrival there of Gillon's former ship *South Carolina,* which had become a British prize). He received reports on the number of likely participants in the expedition (the size was wildly exaggerated, but probably referred to a different plan than the one that finally emerged), the likely leader of the affair (a reported militia colonel), and the timing for such an attack.[9] Other sources of information corroborated the disturbing news from St. Augustine.

Truce ships were another of those factors that caused Claraco to look apprehensively toward Florida. The Spaniards relied heavily on truce, or flag, ships to bring back all types of vital intelligence. Since the official mission of these ships involved such tasks as exchanging prisoners, delivering stranded sailors, moving families, and communicating official requests, New Providence had numerous opportunities to send these vessels wherever its Spanish governors wished. Until the winter of 1782 Claraco and Andrés directed most of their flags to Charleston, certainly not the closest British port but clearly the one with the most enemy activity. After Charleston's evacuation in December 1782 these truce ships went to St. Augustine.[10] It was understood by all sides that these ships returned home with intelligence. What Claraco and Andrés found so disturbing about the flags sent to St. Augustine was that British officials detained these ships in Florida after 1 January 1783—a sure sign that someone at the other end wanted certain news kept secret.[11]

Such a conclusion was even more believable when combined with the conduct of many residents of Nassau, who had their own sources of information from Florida. By February 1783 numerous individuals had asked the governor's permission to leave Nassau immediately, some to reside on nearby islands and others to live

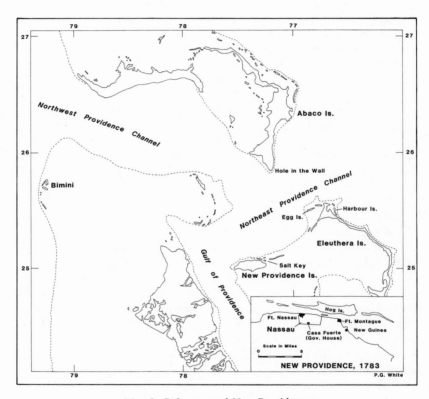

Map 3. Bahamas and New Providence

temporarily in the interior of New Providence. Several citizens sought to shift their lodgings from areas close to the main fort to houses on the edge of the capital. Some islanders even requested instructions from the Spaniards on how they should conduct themselves if the Bahamas were invaded. A few asked the governor to return property lent or rented to the Spaniards, fearful that a Spanish defeat would result in the loss of these goods. Only the most obtuse of officers, which Claraco was not, could have failed to understand that something was afoot.[12]

The stirrings in St. Augustine, however, resulted primarily from the events of the moment. With so many soldiers and refugees congregating in East Florida, and with the likelihood that St. Augustine would not be attacked by either the Spaniards or the American rebels, pressure mounted on British officials to employ this force constructively—that is offensively. The most logical targets did not necessarily include the Bahamas. Spanish West Florida and Louisiana seemed to be more attractive objectives. Both of these colonies were lightly populated and could be used to provide refuge for loyalists fleeing lost British possessions further north. The regular military officers in St. Augustine hence turned their attention to planning an operation against Pensacola and New Orleans.[13] Although there were general orders to recapture the Bahamas, only an unofficial or private venture against the Spaniards in Nassau had any chance of gaining adherents in St. Augustine.[14]

Support for an irregular strike came from two different sources, both essential to a successful attempt on New Providence. The first group interested in such a project was a number of Bahamian refugees living in St. Augustine, the most important among them Robert Rumer.[15] Rumer, a resident of Harbour Island, one of the Out Islands in the Bahamas, had fled to East Florida sometime after the Spanish conquest of New Providence in May 1782. He and several other Bahamian exiles sought to persuade Governor Patrick Tonyn of East Florida to employ the excess British soldiers and naval forces around St. Augustine against Nassau, arguing that it was the crown's duty to liberate subjects forced to endure the "oppressive" rule of the Spaniards. It was probably the rumors of Rumer's proposal to Tonyn, particularly the estimates of how many troops should be involved, that first reached Spanish spies.

When Tonyn offered little encouragement, Rumer looked elsewhere for his army. Rumer and his associates had much to contribute to someone who would organize this venture. They could provide excellent intelligence on the state of the Spanish garrison in Nassau and how best to attack it. They could also provide financial incentives to those willing to risk their lives. Most importantly, they could contribute manpower. Rumer had access to local corsairs whose participation was absolutely vital to any private venture. Many of these individuals were Rumer's personal friends. Rumer further had contacts with islanders who would be willing to join the expedition once it got as far as the Bahamas. Without the cooperation of influential local leaders few residents of the islands would expose themselves to the risks of helping an invasion force whose origins and commanders were unknown, and which lacked the weight of official British sponsorship. A small expedition and a raiding party looked very much the same. Rumer found his military leader in the person of Andrew Deveaux, a South Carolina militia officer who was at loose ends in St. Augustine.

Deveaux was a twenty-four-year-old loyalist who had arrived in East Florida in December 1782 along with numerous other refugees from Charleston.[16] Forced initially to serve as an officer in the rebel militia of his home town of Beaufort, South Carolina, Deveaux joined the British ranks in early 1779 when a small detachment of His Majesty's soldiers under General Augustine Prevost swept north along the coast from Savannah toward Charleston. Deveaux went on to enjoy modest success as a partisan campaigner in the rugged and often brutal struggle for the southern countryside during the 1780s.

Deveaux's rather cavalier willingness to bend the rules of warfare, undoubtedly learned in the bitter battles for the Carolinas and Georgia, would stand him in good stead in the Caribbean. Because of his zeal, ability, and family connections the South Carolinian held two British commissions in his home state. The first came from Lord Cornwallis and assigned Deveaux the rank of captain commandant of a loyalist regiment of provincials called the Royal Foresters. Deveaux never succeeded in fully mobilizing this unit because too many of the original members were killed by the enemy. His second commission was that of major in the Granville County Loyalist Militia, a very active regiment whose colonel was Deveaux's brother-in-law, Lieutenant Colonel Nicholas Lechemere. Lechemere, one suspects, had much to do with his Deveaux in-laws becoming loyalists. The lieutenant colonel was a civil servant in Beaufort and would obviously lose his post if the royal government fell. Deveaux's South Carolina reputation was almost entirely forged as a member of the latter group. The first commission, however, would be the one resurrected for the Bahamas since provincial troops were several steps above militia in the pecking order of military observers. Deveaux could also usurp the rank of colonel for the provincials, the traditional grade for officers in charge of a regiment.

Deveaux supported himself as a soldier in South Carolina from the fruits of captured booty, accumulating a respectable estate before going into exile. After reaching St. Augustine, he saw no reason to give up his accustomed source of income. He immediately organized a raid along the Georgia coast to sink or capture rebel shipping. He also toyed with the idea of participating in a planned operation against Pensacola. However, the proposal to lead an attack in person on the Bahamas seemed too attractive to pass up. Deveaux had never commanded an operation of this size and complexity. Nevertheless, he was a veteran, held a commission to lead men, was available, and promised to bring along a number of loyalists who had served with him around Charleston. He also had some personal money to invest in the venture, claiming afterward to have used nearly £5,000 of his own funds in the expedition, almost surely an exaggerated figure. After the war enthusiastic historians elevated Deveaux to a pantheon of war heroes which included Drake, Wolfe, and Montgomery. They described the South Carolinian as a military genius who comes along only once or twice a century and a person whose character was "restless and daring."[17] Before April 1783, however, Deveaux's talents and reputation were far more ordinary than this.

With Rumer's help the South Carolinian began to prepare his private expedition in February 1783. What Rumer and Deveaux were able to assemble in St. Augustine was hardly very encouraging or impressive. Deveaux collected seventy loyalist veterans and expected that several dozen more would join him at sea on the passage to the Bahamas.[18] The terms under which these men enlisted were unclear. One group of prospective volunteers had an agreement with Deveaux in which the commander provided arms and provisions in return for their services. Should the venture end victoriously, the volunteers would also receive a share of the prizes and the promise of land in the Bahamas.[19] Deveaux further offered the post of second in command to the person who brought with him the most followers. Since Deveaux later signed another agreement which in effect nullified this accord, particularly the part as to how booty was to be divided, it is difficult to say whether any written understanding existed for most participants.[20]

While the number of soldiers who followed Deveaux from St. Augustine was scant, the naval arm of the expedition had more substance. Deveaux and Rumer enlisted six transports to ferry their small army and supplies to the Bahamas. In addition, two formidable corsairs—the *Perseverance*, a 26-gun brigantine under Thomas Dow, and the *Whitby Warrior*, a 16-gun brigantine with a 120-man crew under Daniel Wheeler—escorted the expedition to its destination. Two other vessels, smaller but heavily armed, sailed along as well. Later in the enterprise some additional large corsairs would participate.[21] All these English privateers gave the undertaking control of the sea around Nassau but not in the capital's harbor. The sea force from St. Augustine was adequate for the task ahead; the land force was not. Deveaux and Rumer banked heavily on fleshing out their thin ranks with manpower in the Bahamas.

The transports slipped out of St. Augustine on Monday, 30 March, and picked up their corsair escort off the St. Augustine bar on 1 April. Together they set sail for the southwest Bay of Abaco, the designated rendezvous point. The entire expedition almost disintegrated before reaching the Bahamas when two large ships bearing "foreign colours" bore down upon the convoy. Outgunned, the escort ships beat an embarrassing retreat, leaving the lumbering transports and Deveaux to their fate. Fortunately the enemy vessels turned out to be English ships returning from Jamaica who were looking for easy spoils along the way.[22] After exchanging news with the English ships, the small flotilla proceeded, reaching Abaco the following Monday and finding the corsair escorts awaiting them. A council of war was held to discuss how best to recruit local Bahamians for the campaign ahead. The advice and assistance of islanders were vital to completing this crucial task.

Posting guard ships so that word of the expedition would not reach the garrison at Nassau, the flotilla proceeded to Harbour Island. At Harbour and Eleuthera, the two most heavily populated Out Islands in the Bahamas at this time, recruiters rounded up volunteers. The names and number of those enlisted are not known since Deveaux ran the undertaking more like a partisan raid than a regular military operation. Nevertheless, recruiters evidently took almost every man capable of bearing arms from Harbour Island and somewhat fewer from Eleuthera. The total was close to 170 men, with approximately 120 from Harbour and 50 from Eleuthera.[23] A 1782 census for the Bahamas listed 90 residents capable of bearing arms living on Harbour Island out of a population of 179 males (97 whites, 2 mulattoes, and 80 blacks). Eleuthera reportedly had 120 men of military age from a total adult population of 146 males (102 whites, 21 mulattoes, and 23 blacks). Robert Rumer, who played a crucial role in the recruiting, estimated that they took nine-tenths of those who could fight—a figure that was probably true for Harbour Island but not for Eleuthera.[24]

These Bahamian reinforcements came from all three racial groups, with whites predominating only because there were more of them. Evidence suggests, however, that blacks and mulattoes served a longer time and may have been the dominant racial groups at the end of the campaign.[25] Although Deveaux sought volunteers, there was some intimidation, even threats of retribution, against those who might wish to sit this affair out.[26] With the addition of these 170 Bahamians, Deveaux's army numbered nearly 300 men, including sailors who could be detached from the corsairs. This total would increase still more once the invaders reached the most populated island, New Providence.

Because Deveaux needed several days to train and arm the additions to his army, he moved his force to Egg Island. While there the corsairs captured several ships sailing to and from Nassau.[27] They also made contact with key individuals in the capital, notifying them about what was to happen and soliciting information on the state of Spanish defenses. Deveaux had excellent intelligence on Spanish weaknesses. It also seems quite likely that he learned at Egg Island what the Spaniards had just discovered—that a preliminary peace accord had been signed in January and that the war was over.[28] Ignoring this last piece of information, if indeed he ever received it, on 12 April Deveaux moved his force one last time to Salt Key, just a few miles east of Fort Montague.

Until 12 April 1783 the Spaniards were ready and waiting for the Deveaux expedition, or any other, to appear. There were so many signs pointing toward an attack that Governor Claraco worked feverishly to prepare his defenses. The governor issued several urgent appeals for help to Cuba. He extracted as much labor as he could from his troops to improve the island's fortifications. The harbor of Nassau was shut down in order to keep information from enemy cruisers. Fort Montague received reinforcements, and its commander had instructions for its defense should the British assault it. Claraco warned local leaders that he held them responsible for the conduct of the civilian population. He expected them to keep a count of the male population and to ensure that locals stayed neutral during a siege. The governor also demanded that island officials identify potential hostages to make certain that residents behaved themselves.[29] Had Deveaux moved his attack up a few days, he would have found a very tough, probably impossible, situation confronting his forces. By the end of the day on 12 April, however, the Spaniards abandoned their extraordinary defense measures. What led the Spaniards to turn their backs on a dangerous enemy when the threat was the greatest can only be understood within the context of information reaching Nassau.

On 10 April a ship from Havana arrived in New Providence with the latest correspondence from the new governor of Cuba, Luis de Unzaga.[30] Considering Deveaux's actions to isolate New Providence, it was remarkable that this vessel got through. She did, however, without encountering any hostile ships. The Spanish sloop, which must have been *La Flor del Mayo*, had left Cuba on 3 April and brought a letter dated 2 April from Unzaga to Claraco.[31] This April 2 letter went a long way toward deciding the ensuing struggle in favor of the English.

Unzaga responded to Claraco's urgent pleas for assistance by informing the Bahamian governor that unofficial word had just reached Havana from Cape François that peace had been declared. Equally important Unzaga reported that New Providence was to revert to English control and that Florida was returned to Spanish suzerainty. He ordered Claraco to prepare for these changes immediately by taking inventories of government goods and supplies in order to expedite a prompt evacuation of Nassau. At the first opportunity he was to turn the colony over to properly appointed representatives of the English government. The war was over. The Spaniards wanted to stay in the Bahamas no longer than was necessary. The danger of corsairs was now past, and Nassau had proven to be a very expensive outpost.

Between 10 and 12 April Claraco put his new orders into effect. He stopped work on the fortifications of Nassau, and the garrison was released from the alert it had been maintaining for several weeks. On 12 April, except for a dozen soldiers, the detachment at Fort Montague was called back to Nassau, where it was easier and cheaper to billet troops. Claraco opened the port to traffic.[32] Little did Claraco, a professional soldier, know that he would soon face the problem of fighting during peacetime for a colony no longer Spanish. Deveaux, whose military schooling was that of a Carolina partisan, would not find the situation too great a dilemma.

If Deveaux had not learned about the peace at Harbour Island, he most certainly heard about it at Salt Key, where dozens of individuals from Nassau began to visit him. The Spaniards had no reason to keep such welcome news from the general public in New Providence, and everyone noticed the change in alert status of the garrison. Nevertheless, Deveaux chose to ignore this information —and he would ignore it again when told in person by Claraco. Eighteenth-century peace negotiators always had a perplexing problem in setting an exact date to end hostilities. If too short a grace period was fixed between the peace accord and the end of hostilities, nations ran a risk that many would not receive the news in time, resulting in some continuing to fight while others had stopped. If too long a grace period was allowed, however, other problems emerged that were equally grave in nature, including the temptation to try one last campaign despite the danger of upsetting the peace agreements.

The Paris Peace Preliminaries, signed in January 1783, had stipulated a two-month grace period, with fighting ending everywhere on 9 April. Sufficient as this period might have seemed in January, official news of the accord had not yet reached Deveaux by April 1783. Indeed, it apparently had not yet arrived in East Florida, although it soon would.[33] Anticipation of just such news, however, was prevalent almost everywhere in the New World. Deveaux and his apologists always dismissed the peace news that the militia colonel received from the Spaniards as "trifling information," not worth believing even though the enemy showed by their actions that they obviously believed it. Historians, however, cannot ignore the fact that Deveaux and others had invested considerable funds and time in this expedition. All would be lost if they stopped or turned back. The twelfth of April was already three days past the date to end hostilities. The war continued in the Bahamas while armies stacked weapons elsewhere.

Although the Spaniards no longer maintained a high-level alert, they did continue normal military vigilance, and the presence of Deveaux at Salt Key could hardly have gone unnoticed for long.

On 12 April, and particularly on 13 April, lookouts to the east sighted unusual ship activity near Fort Montague.[34] Several vessels were spotted as they were visited by fishing boats and other small craft from New Providence. John Ferguson, a prominent businessman in Nassau who had petitioned to leave Nassau and had received permission to do so, reported to Claraco that he had two ships at Harbour Island waiting for him and his possessions. He asked the governor's approval to visit these vessels and bring them into port.[35] Once again luck ran with the audacious attackers lurking on the fringe of New Providence. At one of those points in history where several different conclusions could have been drawn, Claraco interpreted these events to mean that a serious effort to introduce contraband into Nassau was about to get under way.

There were a number of reasons for Claraco to reach such a supposition. The fact that peace had been declared was the most persuasive. Although Claraco had just found out about it, there was little reason to suppose that the British did not also know. British supremacy on the high seas, though severely tested during the war, usually meant that English colonies had better communication with Europe than did the Spaniards. Reinforcing this logical, but erroneous, conclusion was the information that the governor had received from St. Augustine earlier in the year. Any British attack on New Providence was to have been a major expedition of one to two thousand troops escorted by large ships of the line. The small vessels sighted by the watch and visited by New Providence fishermen could hardly be the advance guard of anything so serious as an invasion. Claraco's own experience in Nassau contributed to his miscalculation. Contraband trade was a way of life for many Bahamian merchants. Goods brought in before the Spaniards left had two potential markets. Local sellers might be able to entice part of the retiring garrison to take some merchandise home to trade in the rich Havana market. Moreover, the return of British control, which almost certainly meant the stationing of small army units in Nassau, also opened the door for some handsome profits in New Providence itself.

The preparations which Claraco made on 13 April were designed to stop illegal trade, not an invading army. Suspecting that the effort to run contraband would be made during the night or early morning of 13–14 April at New Guinea, a small village east of Fort Montague where the *Garland* had, months before, tried to land her party of sailors, Claraco reinforced the garrison at the eastern fort with ten more soldiers. This bastion had a token detachment of eighteen men (fifteen soldiers plus three artillery men) under a junior officer (*subteniente*), José de Retes. On the night of 13 April the troop allotment at the fort was twenty-eight men. Claraco next took two of the longboats from the three Spanish patrol boats anchored off Fort Montague and sent them with an armed contingent of sailors to keep a surveillance off the coast for smugglers. The regular sea watch was also augmented with additional sailors. The garrison at Fort Montague sent two patrols down the coast toward New Guinea during the evening and blocked the land road to the village from Nassau with a sentinel. Another group of sailors from the patrol boats went to the outskirts of New Guinea itself to await the smugglers. What was left of the crews in the anchored boats (a skeletal complement of a few men each) and the garrison were alerted to prevent the suspected criminal activity. Should the night patrols fail to discover anything, Claraco had arranged for an officer from Fort Nassau to make a reconnaissance to Harbour Island early the next day with a felucca full of armed sailors.[36] If smugglers had approached New Providence from the east on 13 April, they would have been stopped and most likely apprehended.

Deveaux and his army were ready by 13 April. Even though the colonel expected more men from East Florida at any moment, he dared not wait too much longer. The attackers' plan was to strike at Fort Montague simultaneously by land and sea early in the morning of 14 April, hoping to catch the garrison and ship crews asleep or unprepared and befuddled. The eastern fort had been the weakest spot in New Providence's defense throughout the war and was the first target for every invader. Deveaux possessed the latest intelligence on the state of the fort's vigilance from a number of early morning fishermen who made a point of leaving for their supposed run from the fort.[37] Although the British would hardly catch anyone napping, they could not have hoped for a greater surprise.

With so many Spanish patrols looking for smugglers, it seems astonishing that no alarm reached Fort Montague about the impending assault until the very last moment, too late to put up an effective resistance. After the attack Spanish officers themselves struggled to understand how the British escaped detection. Much of the explanation, however, can be attributed to the amazing luck of the attackers and to the failure of the Spaniards to recognize the unexpected.

Claraco logically assumed that any smuggling party would try to avoid the fort, and hence his patrols looked for their prey at some distance from the garrison. Yet it was precisely the fort that was the target. In the case of the sea patrols, one was captured while another stumbled across the British off New Guinea, got involved in a confused firefight, landed, and fled into the bush. Not until these sailors straggled back to the fort early in the morning of 14 April to find it surrounded by enemy forces did they realize that it was an army and not a large group of smugglers that they had tangled with earlier. For some reason the sounds of their encounter with the British did not reach any other patrol or the fort. The third sea patrol went out and came back having sighted nothing. Since this third patrol arrived back at its ship only an hour before the assault began, one might question the diligence with which it carried out its assignment. As for the land patrols, they went out too far from the fort looking for contraband. Upon returning to their quarters on the morning of the fourteenth, the last two patrols sighted the enemy preparing his assault. One patrol made it back to the fort only yards ahead of the attackers; the other was chased into the underbrush.[38]

It was really up to the fort itself to sound the alarm. Yet even here circumstances conspired to disguise the British intentions until the very last moment. Retes had the few soldiers not out on patrol on full alert throughout the night. The sounds of the short encounter at New Guinea had not reached Montague. Even by early morning it was still too soon to be concerned about the patrols that had not returned. They were not overdue. At the last critical moment before daybreak the limited manpower of the fort was diverted by the arrival of the felucca sent from Nassau by the governor to make a probe down the coast toward Harbour Island.[39] The slow match for the fort's guns, constantly lit in order to be available for any emergency, was sent to the felucca to enable its crew to start its own match.

At this point the seaward sentry spotted a number of small boats making for the fort. Since these were mainly fishing boats, the type of vessel that might run contraband, no alarm was sounded to warn of an impending attack. Instructions, however, were shouted to the three anchored patrol boats off the fort to force the suspicious craft alongside for inspection. This the patrol boats did. Using Minorcan settlers from East Florida to answer in clear Castilian that they would come alongside, the fishing boats swept in beside two of the three anchored ships.[40] By the time that the Spanish deck officers realized that these craft were full of men, it was too late. Two of the three Spanish vessels fell to the British with only one casualty, a Spanish captain who tried bravely to train a swivel gun on the boarders only to be wounded by a pike for his endeavors. The crew and captain of the third Spanish patrol boat abandoned ship, not having the hands needed to get it under way and finding their guns pointed shoreward instead of toward their sister, now enemy, ships.[41] It was evident to the fort that something more serious than smuggling was afoot.

Seeing what had happened, Retes looked frantically for the missing match so he could fire on the captured ships in front of the fort, a fruitless search since the match had been removed to the felucca, which had fled back to Nassau. Then a landward sentry and a returning patrol brought word that assault troops were approaching the fort from the east.[42] Facing Retes were some 170 men, plus nearly 70 more that had swarmed over the captured vessels in the harbor. Had all of Retes's twenty-eight soldiers been on hand, which they were not, he could not have held Fort Montague. The young officer quickly made plans to flee, and he was lucky to have escaped without being captured.

Claraco's standing instructions for the commander of Fort Montague were to warn Nassau of an attack by firing the fort's guns, to hold out as long as feasible, and then to retreat toward the city.[43] During this last maneuver the commander was to blow up the fortress, rendering it useless to the enemy. The governor had ordered that shafts be dug under two sections of the walls in anticipation of the need to destroy Montague. These mines were packed with powder and had only to be lit.

Retes tarried at the fort long enough to organize the departure of the garrison, ordering it to leave one by one so as to present a smaller front to enemy fire, and to light a new match to ignite the fuses for the two mines. Had Deveaux moved quicker, the British could have seized the entire garrison. As it was, only the last two Spanish soldiers in the fort, a sentry and a sergeant, fell into British hands before they could leave. One of these was intimidated into cutting the fuses to the mines, preventing the destruction of the fort. The disappearance of the original match, which

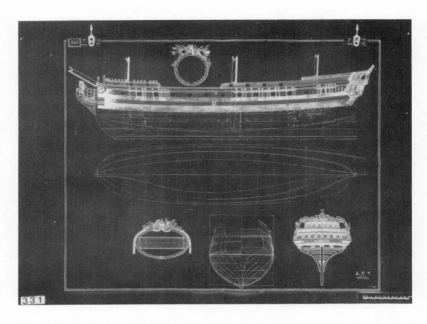

Illustration 2. Design of the frigate *South Carolina* in 1779. Note that the ship had not yet changed its name from *L'Indien* to *South Carolina*. From Archivo Histórico Nacional, Madrid.

Illustration 3. Col. Andrew Deveaux, Jr. Artist unknown. Courtesy of the Public Record Office, Nassau.

kept the fort from firing its cannon to warn Nassau, and the failure of the mines to go off generated suspicion later among the Spaniards that they were the victims of treason by one of their soldiers at the fort, an erroneous but understandable supposition.[44] Whether or not there were Spanish traitors, the assault on New Providence had begun.

With the unequal contest for Fort Montague over, the struggle for the capital began. Although the Spanish garrison at the fort had been unable to warn their comrades of the attack, the British inadvertently did so by firing the cannons of the captured Spanish ships at the fleeing garrison. The sounds of battle put Claraco on notice that something was happening. Shortly thereafter stragglers arrived from the east, although some of the Montague garrison did not find their way to Spanish lines until the following day. Had Deveaux pressed his advantage once again, he might have ended the contest in a day. Instead the English, surprised at the ease of their success, paused to regroup and to consider their next step. This respite gave the Spaniards plenty of time to react.

At this point in the campaign, the two sides were almost equal in size. The loss of the fort and three ships was a serious blow to the Spaniards. Just as important for the defenders was the question of health. A sizeable percentage of the garrison had been sick during the month of April; the military hospital had reported an average of nearly fifty patients a day.[45] Nevertheless, the Spaniards still controlled Nassau and four patrol boats, and had lost little of their garrison since so few had been captured at Fort Montague.[46]

Yet the odds were shifting. Deveaux's forces were growing with the addition of numerous fishermen from New Providence.[47] Most importantly, Deveaux knew exactly where his foe was and how many Spaniards he faced. The reverse was not true. Surrounded by a hostile population, Claraco had no reliable source of information on the English forces. Those who had collaborated with the Spaniards now looked for ways to leave the island and found themselves isolated from the rest of the population. Some of those who had provided valuable intelligence to Claraco previously now tried to project an image of neutrality by avoiding contact with the garrison. One possible source of news for the Spaniards was captured enemy soldiers; but the chance of taking captives was slim for the Spanish defenders.

Spanish ignorance about the English forces began to play an

increasingly important role as events unfolded. Many traditional accounts of the siege of Nassau laud Deveaux's genius at deceiving the Spaniards about his real strength. The English commander supposedly did this in many ways. He purportedly planted straw dummies along his lines to give the impression of more manpower than he had. He reportedly achieved the same impression by having skiffs move back and forth from ship to shore with men lying down one way and sitting up the other to suggest a steady stream of reinforcements reaching land. As part of Deveaux's effort to outsmart Claraco, he supposedly employed a few Indians and war whoops (a loyalist twist to the Boston Tea Party story) to strike terror into the hearts of the defenders.[48] As entertaining and romantic as most of the alleged actions are, they received little mention in the English primary sources, which consist primarily of Deveaux's letters. Particularly intriguing is the nearly complete absence of reports concerning these events in the very exhaustive Spanish accounts of the siege.[49] That the Spaniards misjudged the size and quality of Deveaux forces is certain, although Deveaux's followers would eventually number as many, if not more, as the besieged garrison. Why the Spaniards miscalculated so badly had nothing to do with enemy tricks and deceptions. Instead, it had everything to do with Spanish intelligence gathering.

All reports from St. Augustine had insisted that the impending attack would include a substantial number of regular troops drawn from the retired garrison of Charleston. Even the precise number to expect (1,500 to 2,000 soldiers, the same numbers that the Spaniards thought sufficient in 1782) made its way back to Claraco. Deveaux was careful to show himself and the few trained militia (the so-called Royal Foresters) that he had in their proper uniforms. The English colonel knew how little respect volunteers would inspire among the professional soldiers on the other side. With no information to contradict Claraco's impression that he was indeed facing the invasion that he had been warned about, the Spanish governor and his fellow officers assumed logically, but incorrectly, that they were badly outnumbered.

While Deveaux had no superiors to answer to, Claraco did. Governor Unzaga's instructions of 2 April influenced Claraco's actions from the moment the invasion started, and they proved to be a serious impediment to his reacting aggressively against the British. Unzaga had ordered Claraco to turn New Providence over to the first authorized British official to appear. These were instructions that superseded previous directions to defend the colony. New Providence was to be returned in the same condition that it had been when Spain acquired it in 1782. All Deveaux had to do was to present the proper credentials and New Providence was his without a fight. Claraco was trained to obey orders and apparently never comprehended that he was dealing with a private army to whom it mattered greatly how the colony was returned to British authority. Military conquest meant fame and booty, while a peaceful transition of authority meant nothing to Deveaux's soldiers of fortune. Even if it had, Deveaux and company would not have been the officials picked by their government to restore the British presence in the Bahamas.

Claraco's indecision over the next couple of days showed his extreme confusion as to the best response to the crisis he faced. In a sense two different military traditions were involved. Claraco represented one forged in European conflicts where professional armies and officers had a common code of conduct, while Deveaux epitomized another molded in the guerrilla battles of the Carolinas where the only rule was not to lose. Defeat meant the loss of everything to Deveaux. Each indecisive step by Claraco only emboldened Deveaux and made the Spanish position ever more precarious.

Once Claraco determined what had happened at Fort Montague, a process that took several hours on the morning of 14 April, he immediately attempted to arrange a meeting with the English leader in order to notify him that peace had been declared. The Spanish governor did manage to contact Deveaux later that day, and presented him with copies of letters received from Havana, including that of 2 April. Deveaux dismissed the peace reports in these communications as "trifling," nothing more than an attempt to buy time—which in one sense it was.[50] The time that Claraco wanted, however, was not to increase his ability to defend the island. He wanted a lull so that final or official word on the peace could reach Nassau. When it was apparent that the Spaniards were not going to surrender immediately, Deveaux was willing for reasons of his own to meet the Spanish governor to discuss a truce. As it turned out, Deveaux also wanted a respite from hostilities, but not one that was too long.

The English colonel needed time to reorganize his forces, to await reinforcements expected from St. Augustine, and to rest his exhausted troops, most of whom had gotten little sleep the night before. However, Deveaux was not interested in a long suspension of hostilities, since this might result in official word of peace arriving. As much as Deveaux evaded the issue of whether he knew that peace had or had not been declared, an official announcement in his hands or in those of Claraco would end the campaign. On 14 April, with both commanders trying to sort out what the future promised, Deveaux and Claraco signed a truce. This temporary agreement provided for a boundary between the forces (a large fig tree halfway between Nassau and Fort Montague served as the dividing mark), a formal guard of twenty-five men from both sides to ensure that no one crossed the line, and an exchange of boats to serve as a guarantee of honorable conduct by the two opponents. It also set a limit on the activity of American ships that might arrive in Nassau during the truce and an expiration date (20 May) after which armed conflict could be resumed.[51]

Both sides had cause to be satisfied with the agreement. Claraco could hardly have expected a longer truce period; the twentieth of May was more than sufficient for news about the peace preliminaries to arrive in the proper form. On the other hand Deveaux had gained a significant victory for his side. He had no intention of honoring this agreement any longer than necessary. In the meanwhile he held the Spanish boats in the harbor as hostages to the truce, and had neutralized Claraco's relatively fresh forces. A slip of paper stopped a potential Spanish counterattack at a time when it could have been most dangerous.

Less than twenty-four hours later, Deveaux found an excuse to terminate the truce. Claraco and Deveaux had scheduled a meeting for 15 April at 10:00 A.M. to exchange copies of their agreement. Deveaux did not show up. When he finally contacted the Spanish commander later in the day, he accused the Spaniards of violating the truce by sending patrols past the boundary line, a charge that none of the contemporary documents supports. He also justified his renunciation of the accord by charging that the Spaniards had continued to improve their defenses,[52] a complaint with substance but one that certainly did not violate the truce. In fact, the British had done much the same thing themselves. It was not in Deveaux's interest to grant more time to the Spaniards. The odds had shifted decisively in his favor, but the militia colonel had to move fast.

Hindered by his miscalculations regarding the number of English troops that he faced and hurt by his indecisiveness in interpreting Unzaga's orders of 2 April, Claraco decided to stand on the defensive against his English adversaries. Some of the governor's junior officers and naval advisers wanted to retake Fort Montague and believed that Deveaux had revealed his youth and inexperience by halting after seizing Montague.[53] Disregarding their views, the governor issued directives on 16 April to scuttle the remaining Spanish ships in the harbor and transfer their crews to land fortifications. Thus, the English gained control of the harbor without a fight. Claraco had previously decided to consolidate his troops in the capital by stationing them in the *Casa Fuerte*, the citadel that had been constructed around the governor's house overlooking the city.

These passive tactics were to have a disastrous result. First of all, a number of Americans who had volunteered to help retake Fort Montague despaired of victory and fled the island, diminishing Claraco's manpower.[54] More significant was the abandonment of most of the capital to the British. Nassau's population, sensing the possibility of a Spanish defeat, felt free to participate. Some of the city's residents fled to ships in the harbor or to the interior for the duration of the battle, hoping to avoid involvement. A good portion, however, joined the attackers. Included in this number was the bulk of the island's former militia led by Robert Sterling.[55] If Claraco had bothered to take civilian hostages as he had threatened to do at other times, civilian support for the invaders might have been prevented.

The overpowering foe that Claraco always felt he faced now became a reality. Claraco's decision to consolidate his forces in the citadel made sense from one point of view, but it eventually limited the number of Spanish troops available to the defenders. The total of Spanish soldiers sick and unfit for duty mounted rapidly because the ill and healthy were crowded together in the citadel. Tasks for which the governor had formerly hired locals (preparation of food, drawing water, and nursing the sick) were now done by the soldiers themselves, diminishing those available for fighting. Several dozen Spanish merchant seamen took refuge in the *Casa Fuerte*. Although potentially bodies to strengthen the defense, in practice they added little but confusion. Lastly, the *Casa Fuerte* itself had glaring weaknesses that sapped the spirit of the defenders. Spanish gun emplacements had been constructed in such a way that they set their wooden casemates on fire when used. The citadel's well was located outside the walls, and water runs proved to be a major task involving much of the garrison. Most remarkable, considering Claraco's own training in fortifications, several nearby hills overlooked the

Casa Fuerte. Under the leadership of Robert Rumer, local Bahamians fortified some of these heights with batteries of their own, subjecting the citadel to devastating fire.[56]

Ensconced in their hilltop fortress, the Spaniards reconnoitered British positions. Those patrols that were sent, rarely more than a noncommissioned officer plus four men, seldom went far since these squads had to pass through a maze of city streets, full of dangerous spots for ambushes. One Spanish probe, however, nearly ended Deveaux's life. The colonel escaped death only because two point-blank shotgun blasts misfired.[57] The majority of Spanish forays ended with the patrols being located quickly by the enemy and chased back to the citadel. By 17 April, if not before, Claraco began to despair. In his view, rightly as it turned out, no assistance was coming from Havana. He wondered how long he should fight for a colony that would be turned over to the enemy regardless of the outcome of his efforts. At one point the despondent governor toyed with the idea of blowing up the *Casa Fuerte*, taking the lives of defender and attacker alike, if the enemy breached its walls.[58]

Passive in his defense of New Providence, the Spanish governor yielded also to exhaustion and fear in his decision of 17 April to surrender to the British attackers. Never certain when Deveaux might attempt an assault, Claraco had kept his entire garrison at the walls of the citadel since 14 April. Such an extreme reaction resulted partly from the meetings and messages between Claraco and Deveaux, which ended typically with the English colonel threatening an immediate attack.[59] Taking Deveaux at his word, a dangerous thing to do with the devious South Carolinian, Claraco drained the energy of his troops and officers with an around-the-clock watch. As one of his subordinates pointed out, the Spanish garrison should have had most of its regulars resting in order to mount an effective defense over the long run.[60] Claraco was also worried about what might happen should his lines be overrun. Many residents of Nassau had joined the enemy. Although disciplined troops could be kept under control, the governor was not confident that the local inhabitants of New Providence could be. There were enough private vendettas against the Spanish garrison to make the prospect of a defeat unpleasant to contemplate.

Convening a council of war of his principal officers on 18 April, Captain Claraco explained the need to capitulate and opened the question to discussion.[61] On 18 April 1783 the Spaniards agreed

to surrender New Providence in return for transportation back
to Havana (to Spain in the case of Claraco), the right to maintain
an honor guard of Spaniards at Fort Montague until official word
of peace arrived, and the privilege of marching from the *Casa
Fuerte* with full military honors. All government property became
the possession of the victors, a nice booty if they could sell it. Spanish merchants and civilians were allowed two months to settle their
affairs and leave.[62] Deveaux, who could hardly have pressed for
more, found these terms highly acceptable. After eleven months
and ten days as a Spanish colony, the Bahamas were returned once
again to British rule.

Chapter Six

AFTERMATH

With the exception of the Turks Islands in the far eastern part of the Bahama chain, outposts which had been seized and defended by French troops from St. Domingue just before the end of the war,[1] the Union Jack flew over the major islands of New Providence once again. Although negotiators at the preliminary peace meeting in France had decided to return the Bahamas to Great Britain, the unexpected success of the Deveaux expedition sped up a change of command that would have been slow at best. Just how slow can be gleaned from the history of East Florida, a province which did not welcome its Spanish governor until June 1784. Since East Florida and the Bahamas were geographically close together, it was likely that the exchange of these two colonies would have occurred simultaneously. The final treaty of 1783 granted both possessions the same length of time for a change in masters.[2] Even though the Spaniards were far more anxious to pull their expensive garrison out of New Providence than the English were theirs in St. Augustine, the Deveaux conquest may well have cut a year or more off the Spanish occupation of New Providence. Yet victory brought its own problems to New Providence. With an orderly transfer of power no longer possible, victor and vanquished faced some unexpected difficulties which shaped the future of both.

The most immediate problem for Deveaux was the restoration of a British government. All his experience in partisan war on the continent had not prepared him for the task of administering a province. Loyalist raiders seldom held territory in the Thirteen Colonies long enough to worry about such things. If they did maintain control for any length of time, British superiors provided the government. In the Bahamas lack of experience was compounded by lack of anticipation. Deveaux and his lieutenants had given very little thought to what would happen if the Spaniards surrendered. Most likely Deveaux assumed that local officials would reappear and resume their preconquest duties. This, however, was impossible in Nassau, particularly at the highest level of government. The last British governor, John Maxwell, and his lieutenant governor, James Edward Powell, had been repatriated to England in 1782 by the Spaniards. The King's Council in Nassau, which had so belligerently challenged the authority of previous British governors, was in disarray. Several of its former members were in Havana contending with legal difficulties stemming from their involvement with corsairs. Although records of departures were not kept, others had undoubtedly left the Bahamas for safer territory elsewhere. Of the council members still residing in Nassau at the end of the war, there was no one to lay claim to legitimate authority.[3] Whatever the preference of Deveaux, he had to establish a government until British officials elsewhere relieved him of this duty.

Deveaux revealed his approach to governing the Bahamas within days of the Spanish surrender. He established a committee, called the Board of Police, to rule on a temporary basis. Although the militia colonel could have governed on his own, he was far more interested in reaping the economic spoils of victory before someone else did. Consequently he did not tamper with the affairs of the Board of Police. This committee consisted of seventeen members. Some were administrators from the previous British government. Others came from the class of prominent merchants and citizens residing in New Providence. Still others were important participants in the Deveaux expedition who intended to settle in the Bahamas. The exact number of board members fluctuated, and people who felt that they merited appointment to the committee could apparently join, providing no one objected.[4]

When Deveaux left the Bahamas to carry some of his booty to East Florida in September 1783, the Board of Police continued to operate, but much of its authority came to rest in the hands of Robert Hunt. Hunt was a former member of the island's last council who had recently returned from confinement in Havana.

Hunt and the Board of Police controlled the affairs of the colony until March 1784, when John Maxwell, the governor deposed in May 1782, arrived from England to resume his former duties.

To add to the confusion over who governed in the Bahamas immediately after the war, British officials elsewhere in the Americas attempted to set up their own provisional government for Nassau. Since Deveaux had operated on his own authority, not serving under any immediate superior, Sir Guy Carleton, commander in chief of British land forces in America who was headquartered in New York, decided to appoint his own governor. Having little current knowledge of events in the Bahamas, Carleton ordered Brigadier General Archibald McArthur, then in East Florida, to assume control over Nassau and authorized him to pay Deveaux a pension. McArthur never obeyed these instructions, although he did send a junior officer to the islands twice to report on conditions there. The information supplied by McArthur's aide influenced many loyalists to make the colony their new home.[5]

If there appeared to be a certain helter-skelter quality to the new Bahamian government, there existed a dogged determination by the restored rulers to punish individuals associated with Spanish rule. Those who had suffered the most from the occupation took the lead in this matter. The question was who to punish first. The matter came to a head when Governor Maxwell, still smarting over his embarrassing surrender two years earlier, made public his intention to avenge himself on those Bahamians who had led the victorious Spaniards to the islands in 1782.[6] Maxwell, however, had not lived through the occupation, and most Bahamians with influence had a different target in mind. These persons wanted action taken against citizens who had kept their local positions during the Spanish period and who had not suffered from the crackdown on individuals practicing the corsair trade. In particular they wanted William Bradford, erstwhile member of the King's Council, punished. No reprisals were taken against the pilots who led the Spanish fleet to the Bahamas, even though several evidently stayed in New Providence during and after the Spanish period.[7]

Bradford, however, had been a controversial member of the King's Council in Nassau before the Spanish conquest. He had steadfastly supported several former governors, principally Governor Browne, in their conflict with local residents over smuggling goods into the colony. During the Spanish occupation Bradford had continued to work as official secretary in charge of publishing governmental decrees and other public papers. Since he seemed to have no economic interest in the corsair business, he survived the Spanish suppression of this enterprise; and he countersigned most Spanish proclamations once they had been translated into English. Since the surrender accords of 1782 had specifically encouraged local officials to remain at their posts, there was nothing clearly improper in Bradford's labors. Yet his previous political association with Governor Browne and his relative comfort during the Spanish period made him a prime victim for revenge-minded Bahamians in 1784. These citizens charged Bradford before the island's assembly with dishonesty, neglect of duty, and treason. Bradford was hardly a person that Governor Maxwell felt deserved punishment, but the new governor took no part in defending the secretary. In the end Maxwell accepted Bradford's resignation when it became apparent that the secretary could not avoid censure and removal from office by the assembly.[8]

The task of expelling the unwelcome Spanish garrison was as pressing a problem as that of establishing a local British government. Under more normal circumstances, the Spanish governor in Cuba would either have chartered transport ships to remove the garrison or he would have instructed Claraco in Nassau to contract for vessels to do so. The Deveaux conquest made such an easy transfer of men to Havana impossible. At Fort Montague the British had captured half of the modest Spanish war fleet in the Bahamas. The other Spanish vessels had been run aground during the siege. The ships that had been beached could be salvaged, but only with great difficulty. Those that had been captured, all small in size, were booty of war. To send them to Havana would have been to risk not getting them back, since Cuban officials would have viewed the vessels' seizure as illegal and hence invalid. It would have been equally difficult to get ships from the Deveaux expedition to take defeated soldiers home. As with the captured Spanish ships, those in the Deveaux expedition did not want to risk the ire of Captain General Unzaga in Havana.

Although it was not easy to envision how the Spaniards were going to be removed, it was imperative for military reasons that they leave soon. Deveaux's troops and armada began to disperse almost as soon as the surrender was signed. Some went back to Florida. Others returned to the Out Islands. Many resumed their professions in Nassau and its environs. The predominant body of organized soldiers in New Providence very quickly became the defeated Spanish garrison. Lightly armed and confined to Fort Montague, this was still a dangerous group to allow to linger in the Bahamas any longer than necessary. The temptation to strike at their shrinking enemy might become too great, regardless of the capitulation accords. Indeed, Captain Claraco wrote to Havana in the weeks following the surrender suggesting just a ploy. He pointed out that a small number of soldiers and ships from Havana could easily retake the Bahamas, a proposal that provoked the governor in Havana to wonder why an equally small number of veterans and men-of-war had been unable to hold the islands earlier.[9]

Aside from security considerations there were other reasons to hurry the Spaniards home. It was very difficult to feed the Spanish garrison after the conquest. The American supply of food and other necessities stopped momentarily during the siege and in the weeks following the campaign. An English supply line was slow to develop. The Spanish exchequer in Nassau had no funds to purchase what goods were available, particularly since Deveaux appropriated much of its capital.[10] The local Bahamian treasury was hardly willing to spend its modest resources on the Spaniards. The task of returning the garrison fell primarily by default to former governor Claraco and his military staff.

Using personal funds and the promise of payment in Havana, Claraco formed two small flotillas in May 1783 to transport his force to Cuba. His tiny convoys consisted of a few decrepit Spanish gunboats (so unseaworthy that Deveaux did not consider them worth seizing), several Spanish commercial vessels stranded in the harbor of Nassau during the siege and not viewed as war booty since they were privately owned, and a couple of Dutch and Swedish merchantmen willing to do this type of work.[11] Yet not all the Spaniards in Nassau were fated to return home immediately.

Deveaux's decision to play only a passive role in governing the islands, transferring effective control to a locally dominated Board of Police, presented an opportunity for some to settle scores with the Spaniards. There were still several Bahamian residents imprisoned or residing involuntarily in Havana when the war ended. Among the notable Bahamians yet to return home were John Miller, Alexander Roxbourgh, Robert Hunt, Thomas Roker, and Joseph Hunter. Some on the board felt that the captured garrison offered an opportunity to secure hostages so as to ensure the speedy return of these individuals. Hostages could also serve other purposes. Governors Claraco and Andrés had financed the occupation of the Bahamas in part from confiscated property belonging to those accused of privateering after the conquest in May 1782. The Spanish exchequer had taken careful inventories of what had been expropriated, intending to have records to repay those who could clear themselves of the corsair charges. However, with the Spaniards leaving abruptly in May 1783, there was no guarantee that compensation for this property would be forthcoming. As a result the Board of Police also wanted hostages as a leverage to force settlement of the claims against the Spanish garrison.

At the prodding of the board Deveaux notified Claraco on 5 May, nearly two weeks after the surrender, that he and the principal officers of the Spanish exchequer would not be allowed to depart for Havana until the matters mentioned above were settled.[12] Deveaux's order clearly broke the capitulation agreement that he had signed, and it caught Claraco by surprise. With some sort of warning the Spanish commander and the others could have slipped off the island on the first ships leaving for Havana. Whether his order was legal or not, Deveaux, unsure of and uninterested in his authority over these matters, refused to reconsider his instructions to detain the Spaniards.

Local leaders were specific about whom they wanted retained. In addition to Governor Claraco the board sought the retention of the intendant (Felipe de Yturrieta), the comptroller (Manuel de Cartas), the comptroller of the royal hospital (José Anastacio González), the quartermaster (Antonio Azoños), and the interpreter (Gabriel Sistaré). Except for Sistaré, whose detention was desired so a translator would be available, all of these men had played some role in the confiscation and use of local property. On his own Claraco instructed the chaplain (Miguel O'Reilly) and the sergeant major (Martín de Arias, chief military officer in the garrison after Claraco) to stay behind with the other hapless hostages. Claraco also maintained at Fort Montague an honor guard of sixteen soldiers from the España regiment in case the islands were to be returned briefly to Spanish authority before officially being placed under British control.[13] With the departure of the last soldiers from the garrison in May 1783, there were still some twenty to twenty-five Spaniards in Nassau. A few of these were destined to stay in New Providence far longer than anyone could have guessed.

Meanwhile the local residents who had been detained in Havana straggled back to Nassau over the next year—several later returning to Havana to pursue unfinished legal business concerning their detention during the war. Roxbourgh and Hunt were back in New Providence by September 1783. Miller did not reach Nassau until March 1784. Others found their way home at undetermined dates.[14] All apparently approved of holding hostages in Nassau until the Spanish government satisfactorily responded to their claims. Some felt strongly enough about the issue to communicate their support to the Board of Police while they still resided in Havana, potentially a dangerous thing to do if such letters fell into the wrong hands.[15] What everyone in Nassau failed to realize about their Spanish hostages was that they possessed very little weight or influence in Cuba or in the Spanish colonial government. Claraco was a mere captain in the army, and the exchequer employees were minor functionaries at best. Only in Europe was there real concern about these detainees, and this interest reflected anxiety about the principle of using prisoners of war as security for settling private claims rather than worry over the person of any particular hostage.

In the seventeen months following Deveaux's victory the number of Spaniards in New Providence dwindled. Claraco released his honor guard of sixteen soldiers when it became certain that the Bahamas would not revert to Spanish control, even temporarily. These troops sailed for Havana in September 1783. He also permitted his fellow military officers, soldiers staying because of his command rather than that of the Board of Police, to depart as well. Gradually even Claraco's fellow exchequer officials (he was still the *subdelegado*) shrank in number. At least one escaped from Nassau, and Bahamian authorities released two others, the comptroller and quartermaster, in late 1783. By April 1784, one year after the surrender of New Providence, only three Spanish hostages remained. They were the governor, intendant, and translator. Governor Maxwell sent the latter two back to Cuba in April 1784 to enhance the possibilities of success for one last appeal for compensation by Bahamian merchants.[16] By the summer of 1784 only Claraco still remained in New Providence.

The former governor's detention grew increasingly painful the longer it lasted, becoming almost intolerable when he alone of the garrison was left. Claraco had pinned much of his hope for release upon the reestablishment of a formal British government in Nassau, convincing himself that crown officials would abide by a proper code of conduct regarding prisoners even if local leaders would not. However, the first British governor after the war was John Maxwell, the last ruler of New Providence before the Spanish conquest in 1782. Maxwell had little personal sympathy for a Spaniard who had personally participated in forcing his own humiliating surrender. Nor was Maxwell in a position to push issues that might antagonize local power brokers when he already had enough difficulty with them for other reasons.[17] As a result the British governor did little for Claraco. The former Spanish governor grew increasingly despondent as he realized that no one in Havana was anxious to arrange his release either. Claraco's protector and mentor, Juan Manuel de Cagigal, no longer ruled in Cuba, and his replacement as captain general was not sympathetic toward the appointees of his predecessor. At one point Claraco lamented that he was "a prisoner of peace," forgotten by all and not even accorded the privileges normally granted to captives during wartime.[18]

To add to his troubles Claraco was destitute. For a while after the surrender the Spanish exchequer continued to function in Nassau, receiving modest funds from an occasional Spanish vessel visiting Nassau and from other sources. Hacienda (treasury) officials, however, cleaned out the accounts in November 1783, evidently taking the last pesos with them. Claraco lived for a while on charity and personal credit. Eventually, in 1784, Maxwell agreed to pay the Spaniard a captain's salary, a sum that would be charged against the treasury in Havana.[19] The former governor's psychological state took such a turn for the worse in the summer of 1784—when some residents requested that he be confined to jail rather than enjoy a loose custody which allowed him freedom within the city—that he threatened to shoot any person who laid a hand on him.[20] Compounding the ex-governor's woes was his realization that legal proceedings concerning his administration of New Providence had started in Havana. Unless Claraco could play a personal role in these hearings, his career as a military officer in the Spanish army might be ruined.

On 28 August 1784 Claraco broke his arrest in Nassau and fled the Bahamas, probably by way of Florida. By December 1784 he had reached Havana. It must not be thought, however, that Claraco's escape greatly disturbed British authorities. His captivity had greatly complicated London's relations with Madrid and had not measurably helped Bahamians with claims against the Spanish occupation. Governor Maxwell had orders to end Claraco's irksome detention if it could "with propriety be done."[21] That Maxwell had received these instructions before Claraco escaped is unlikely, but the British governor did not look for his missing hostage once it was clear that Claraco was gone. Nor did the governor inquire into how the Spaniard had fled the Bahamas, an event which had to involve some local assistance.[22]

While the last of the Spaniards slowly left New Providence, the manner in which the British had regained the islands—the conquest taking place days after the truce halting hostilities had gone into effect—guaranteed that there would be diplomatic complications between the respective governments of Deveaux and Claraco. It was a measure of how exhausted each country was from the war that neither side pushed its demands past reasonable limits. The ministers of George III in London and of Charles III in Madrid wanted no cause to revive a war that had taken so long to end. Because of the unofficial nature of the Deveaux expedition on the British side, and because of the relative isolation of the Nassau garrison from other Spanish colonies, it took time before reliable and detailed information about what had happened in the last campaign of the war reached Europe. Once the important facts had been established, however, diplomats became deeply involved.

Spain, being the most aggrieved, took the initiative. The Spanish protest against Deveaux's conduct occurred in two locations. In Europe, Charles III's ambassador in London headed one effort. He wanted a temporary restitution of Spanish control over the Bahamas, compensation for Spanish losses suffered because of the illegal seizure, and an apology from the British government for the misdeeds of its officers in the affair. In the Caribbean, Spanish officials in Havana also made representations to their counterparts in Nassau, pursuing goals similar to those sought by the London ambassador. The European diplomatic activity was in many ways the more important, since it was there that significant trouble could develop should one side be dissatisfied with the final arrangements. Although not as threatening to the general peace, local negotiations in the New World proved to be more interesting and quixotic.

The government of Charles III had a choice of where and how to press the issue of Deveaux. It was possible for the court to make its remonstrations through the British envoy in Madrid. It was also possible to do the same through Bernardo del Campo, the first Spanish representative to the Court of St. James after the cessation of hostilities. Common sense dictated that the latter handle this matter. With the Bahamas once again English, information from Nassau came much faster to London than to any other locale. Indeed, Campo may have received the disturbing news about Deveaux as early as May or June 1783, certainly no later than July, when English newspapers carried accounts of the campaign.[23] By summer Campo's own government wrote him about the subject. Yet it was not until October 1783 that the ambassador felt confident enough of his information to lodge a formal protest with the British court about the loss of the islands.[24] The ambassador's belated note was not unexpected by the royal government. A number of officials had recognized that Deveaux's attack had occurred after the truce date. Like the Spaniards, however, the English had difficulty obtaining trustworthy reports on the particulars of the New Providence campaign.

When the key facts became undeniable in England, particularly the date when Deveaux had commenced his attack, the New Providence conquest turned into a troublesome embarrassment. Initial news of the unexpected expedition and its success had found a very appreciative audience in a country short of good tidings from a disastrous war. Some members of George III's cabinet had even praised Deveaux and his unpretentious army publicly.[25] These sentiments certainly mirrored the opinions of a nation looking for heroes but were difficult to explain to a vexed foreign ambassador. Since popular opinion played a role in eighteenth-century English politics, it would be hard for a ministry to stay in power if it publicly repudiated a war hero that it had a short time before honored. It is understandable that the British government should have moved slowly in deciding on a proper response to Ambassador Campo's protest.

By the spring of 1784 British leaders had reconciled themselves to apologizing in some form for the action of their subjects in seizing the Bahamas. Yet even at this late date, a year after the campaign had taken place, there was considerable hesitation on the part of royal officials to make this an open apology with any substance to it. Campo pressed the British to punish Deveaux directly for his misconduct. Deveaux, however, had prudently disappeared from sight, and the government in London did little to locate him in the morass of migrating loyalists after the war. Domestic politics at court and in parliament made all but the most insipid apology impossible. Moreover, by this time Campo had instructions from his own court to proceed carefully on the Deveaux question and to avoid embarrassing the present cabinet in London.[26] As a result, in the summer of 1785 both courts tacitly agreed to drop the issue. By then the Spanish ambassador had gotten as much satisfaction as he could from the British government—essentially a private expression of regret.[27]

While the cabinet of George III had ceded very little to Campo in this affair, it would have to pay a price elsewhere. The troublesome merchants in Nassau who had been accused of privateering while the colony was under Spanish control now saw their interests sacrificed. In the treacherous bureaucratic and political currents of postwar Havana the Bahamian residents had been able to clear themselves in 1783 of the charges brought against them by the former governor of Cuba, Juan Manuel de Cagigal. These legal victories had been achieved by pushing their cases through the intendant's court in Havana, a setting more hostile to the captain general than to the English enemy. These legal triumphs, however, had been very expensive financially. The Spanish court's decision had the immediate effect of freeing the Bahamians from imprisonment or house arrest in Havana, but it did not have the equally important result of returning the capital and property that had been confiscated in New Providence. This money and property had been used to support the Spanish garrison in New Providence.

There were two ways these assets could have been returned to their former owners. The exchequer in Havana could assign a part of the annual *situado* (subsidy) from Mexico for this purpose. As sympathetic as the intendancy was to the legal case of the Bahamians, since it embarrassed the former governor's men, Intendant Urriza never considered diverting precious currency in Cuba to reimburse foreign entrepreneurs.[28] The other possibility for compensation involved approaching the Spanish court in Madrid. John Miller, one of the best connected of the mistreated merchants and one who had lost a substantial amount of property to the Spaniards, requested the assistance of his government in seeking payment from Spain for his and other Bahamian claims.[29]

As the Spanish government deemed it prudent to press its grievances through its ambassador in London, the British cabinet chose to present Miller's claims through Robert Liston, the British envoy in Madrid. Because of the length and destructiveness of the war, Liston had many merchant claims to settle with the Spanish court, most notably those of British residents in Minorca when that island fell to the Spaniards.[30] Liston was very alert to the political currents at the Spanish court and knew that several principal advisers to Charles III resented the half-hearted apology for the Deveaux expedition proffered by the British government. From the very beginning Liston was not optimistic about achieving a positive result for the New Providence petitioners.

To complicate matters Liston had to explain some undiplomatic actions by Miller. This Bahamian had published and circulated a pamphlet in London about his losses during the war. It was not good etiquette to argue one's case in public before a private decision had been reached. Moreover, Miller's brief publication contained some unkind statements about the character, honor, and integrity of Spanish officials.[31] The fact that Liston's initiative coincided with the Spanish request for an apology concerning Deveaux gave the government of Charles III a suitable means to extract some measure of revenge for the weak British atonement. Madrid rejected the Miller claim, noting sarcastically that he and the other Bahamians would have been compensated for their losses if Deveaux had not illegally destroyed the Claraco administration in Nassau, the only branch of the Spanish government empowered to make these payments.[32]

While court officials wrestled with the Bahama question in Europe, local bureaucrats in the Caribbean were also involved. Considering Deveaux's clear violation of the truce dates set by the preliminary peace treaty, and also considering the overwhelming number of regular troops in Havana at the end of the war, it is interesting to speculate on why the Spaniards did not try to recapture the Bahamas by force. The obvious answer that Spanish officials felt bound by the terms of the truce, even if certain renegade enemy officers did not, and that Cuban leaders felt their court would surely correct the impropriety of Deveaux's campaign, is alone a sufficient explanation. However, it should be noted that the chief military officer in Havana, Captain General Unzaga, was for the moment in a very weak position because of the dismissal of the former governor Cagigal. The strongest administrator in Havana in 1783, and for some time to come, was the Intendant Urriza, a person opposed to any adventure to rescue the army's honor.

Making a strike against New Providence even less likely was the enormous logistical problem facing both the intendant and governor in organizing the return to Europe of a large number of soldiers in Havana. The entire expeditionary army which had been stationed in St. Domingue now descended upon Havana. The Cuban exchequer was insolvent and could hardly find the means to provision these regiments. Military adventurism in the spring of 1783 had no chance of becoming a reality against the background of a depleted Havana treasury. Nevertheless, Cuban leaders did attempt to regain control of the Bahamas by other means.

Since there was sporadic contact between Nassau and Havana in the months after the Deveaux conquest, it was fairly easy for the government in Cuba to monitor events in New Providence. On two occasions the captain general and the intendant sent official delegations from Havana to the islands. Intendant Urriza was responsible for the first commission, but very little is known about it except its purpose and leader, Pedro Mier. Urriza sent Mier to Nassau with instructions to arrest Claraco for certain infractions committed as an official of the exchequer. He was to bring the governor back to Cuba for trial. Mier's mission was part of the continuing struggle in Cuba between the office of the intendant and that of the governor. Claraco's prior arrest and detainment by the Board of Police in Nassau, however, frustrated the objective of Mier's trip.[33] Urriza's desire to bring Claraco to court would have to wait until the former governor returned by other means to Spanish soil.

There was a second Spanish delegation to Nassau after Mier's visit, and the purpose of this group was to reassert Spanish control over the illegally seized colony. Luis de Unzaga, the new captain general in Cuba, approached Raymundo Andrés in July 1783 about traveling to Nassau. Andrés had been Claraco's temporary replacement as governor of New Providence from September 1782 to January 1783, and seemed an obvious emissary to Nassau. Having no orders from Spain to organize such a venture, Unzaga must have reasoned that a sense of honor would lead Bahamian leaders to return the colony to Spanish control.

Andrés accepted his assignment and in August received detailed instructions about his objectives.[34] After securing the transfer of authority to him by local officials, Andrés was to free the Spanish hostages in Nassau and to send them all home under arrest. He was instructed to take testimony from both Spanish and English witnesses concerning the surrender of the islands by Claraco, and he was to solicit complaints from residents against Claraco and other Spaniards in power during the occupation of the Bahamas. Andrés also had a directive to settle accounts with the *armadores* of various corsair ships who had been found innocent of misconduct charges by courts in Havana. In the event that Andrés could not reassert Spanish rule over the Bahamas, he was to recover all Spanish records still in the colony and forward them to Spain. For company and assistance Unzaga assigned Andrés fifteen soldiers, one sergeant, and a hacienda official from the intendant's office. This small Spanish entourage left Havana on 4 September 1783. Seven weeks later Andrés and a few of his companions reached Nassau.

The Andrés voyage seemed ill fated from the beginning. The Spanish ship carrying the delegation, the sloop *Santa Anna*, encountered dangerous weather and currents a short distance from Havana. Taking nearly a month to struggle as far as the Bahama Channel, the *Santa Anna* was blown ashore in the Florida Keys on October 6. What measure of good fortune there was on this voyage manifested itself at this point when the crew was able to save all aboard, along with the ship's cargo and skiff. Andrés promptly sent the skiff to St. Augustine to seek help. In the meantime an American schooner dropped anchor off the wreck on 11 October and agreed to take Andrés and part of his delegation to Nassau, most likely in exchange for permission to sail on to Havana and sell its cargo. Andrés reached Nassau on 24 October and presented his request for a return of the colony to Spanish control.[35]

There was probably no chance that the Andrés mission could have succeeded in Nassau since it was Deveaux and his handpicked successors who were asked to surrender command. Yet Andrés was surely the wrong man to send. His familiarity with the Bahamas, an asset which had recommended him to Unzaga as the best choice for the delegation, also made him unwelcome to residents who had lived through the war. Andrés had been one of the Spanish officers who had enforced confiscation of property against the British *armadores*. Robert Hunt, a Bahamian whose possessions Andrés had sequestered and a person who had spent considerable time imprisoned in Havana, replied to the emissary on behalf of the Board of Police. Hunt refused to allow Andrés ashore and flatly rejected the proposal that the Bahamas be returned to the Spaniards.

After waiting two weeks in the harbor of Nassau hoping in vain for a more positive response, Andrés left New Providence for Havana on 9 November. His only accomplishment had been an exchange of insulting letters with Hunt.[36] By 14 November the governor's envoy and his diminished retinue reached Cuba, empty-handed except for several Spanish detainees whom the Board of Police had released in Nassau. The last hope for the reassertion of Spanish control, slim as it had been, disappeared. When Governor Maxwell assumed his former position in Nassau a short time later, he wrote Unzaga, asking that the Spanish captain general send an officer empowered to settle questions between the two crowns in New Providence. Having done that very thing a short while before, Unzaga ignored Maxwell's letter.[37]

By the end of 1784 memories of the Spanish occupation of the Bahamas had begun to fade for most people. Yet there were two Spanish military officers who could not forget the Bahamas because they faced long and complicated legal proceedings concerning their activities there. One was the former captain general of Cuba, Juan Manuel de Cagigal, whose case was discussed in an earlier chapter. For him the Bahamas was just one of many difficulties. The second officer was Captain Antonio Claraco y Sanz, Cagigal's appointee as governor of New Providence. Claraco's flight from British arrest in August 1784 landed him directly in a Havana prison upon his arrival in Cuba in the late summer or early fall of 1784. Claraco could hardly have known that his Spanish confinement would last until 1791, most of it in the various fortresses of Havana. Whether or not the former governor of the Bahamas had imagined how long this unpleasant part of his life might last, he certainly understood before arriving in Havana that the resumption of his military career would be difficult.

Claraco's new troubles came from two sources, one more dangerous than the other. Strangely enough, no one questioned Claraco's escape from house arrest in Nassau, though he broke his word to his British captors. Nearly all Spaniards viewed his detention as highly improper and unethical, and no official query ever surfaced about circumstances surrounding Claraco's return to Havana. Instead, the most urgent question that Claraco had to resolve stemmed from his surrender of a post to an enemy. Specifically, had he adequately satisfied the demands of military honor in doing so? The second danger confronting Claraco resulted from a continuation of the conflict in Cuba between exchequer and military officials. He was caught in the middle of this bureaucratic struggle. For the moment treasury officials were supreme in Havana; and Claraco, now physically present in Cuba, was within their reach. He had carelessly left himself vulnerable to charges of fiscal misconduct, and the treasury in Havana pressed its legal openings. Claraco could ill afford an adverse court decision in either of his difficulties, especially one condemning his military conduct. Yet it was his problems with the Havana exchequer that initially occupied most of his time in Havana.

It had been the Havana exchequer which caused Claraco's temporary removal from the governorship of New Providence in September 1782. It was also the continuing battle in Havana between the captain general and the intendant which played a role in Claraco resuming his post in January 1783. All the animosity that the intendant's office held for Cagigal's men now focused on Claraco. There were any number of issues that the exchequer could pursue against the former governor of New Providence, but the one selected as the principal example of Claraco's misconduct in Nassau involved a decision that he had made in the heat of battle against the British invaders.

One of the perennial problems faced by eighteenth-century soldiers was the need to keep powder and shot dry. Moisture in an army's arsenal could render any garrison essentially defenseless. In the closing weeks of the Spanish occupation of Nassau, when a possible attack from British Florida seemed likely, Claraco had become concerned about this problem, particularly the need to have dry powder available in all the vulnerable points of his defense. He decided that one ideal container for dry powder was the exchequer's strongbox (*caja fuerte*), the famous Spanish treasury chest of three keys (constructed so that it took three keys, hence three people, each a check on the others, to open). This box was portable, well-constructed, and watertight. Consequently, Claraco requested that the exchequer find a substitute coffer for the money held in the chest, thereby releasing the strongbox for military purposes. The three keys to the *caja fuerte* were held by Claraco (still *subdelegado* of the treasury), Felipe de Yturrieta (treasurer), and Manuel de Cartas (comptroller). Since the latter two officials were on the worst of terms with the governor already, reflecting the attitude of their superiors in Havana, nothing was done about Claraco's request until the day of Deveaux's attack.

In the confusing first hours of the English assault Claraco remembered his need for a safe and dry storage case. He sent for the exchequer officers and their keys to empty the treasury chest of its funds. Only Cartas could be found. Yturrieta was either hiding from the unexpected British attack, avoiding Claraco, or sick

in bed at some unknown location (all explanations given later).
He could not be located. The hard-pressed governor refused to
wait for a thorough search to be made for the treasurer. He ordered his soldiers to force open the chest, to remove the money
to another safe location, and to use the empty money box to store
Spanish powder.[38]

Such instructions broke Spanish treasury regulations, which required that all three key holders be present whenever money was
removed or deposited. Only the most dire emergency could excuse
a failure to comply with this practice. Claraco's decision to flout
these regulations was a serious one that was almost certain to be
investigated after the war. Making the issue more inflammatory
was a surprising discovery made after the siege ended. The funds
that had been removed from the treasury chest did not match the
amount that should have been in the *caja fuerte* according to exchequer records.

In a small treasury like Nassau the amount missing was relatively
modest. Yet given the small salaries of those in charge of New
Providence, all of whom were lower level officials, the difference
between the actual amount and that which should have been there
was substantial. Explanations for the missing funds ranged from
poor and inaccurate accounting practices to outright thievery. In
the former case exchequer officials would be culpable. In the latter
instance there were a number of potential villains, including the
soldiers who guarded the treasure, Claraco and his fellow officers,
and even the treasury officials themselves.

Regardless of what the correct explanation may have been, audi-
tors in Havana had to blame someone for the discrepancy when
they closed the accounts for New Providence. Spanish exchequer
procedures in the eighteenth century did not permit money to
disappear. Private purses would have to make up for misplaced
public funds. In the heated atmosphere of feuding branches of
government it was easy for exchequer officials to fault another part
of the Spanish bureaucracy regardless of the evidence in the case.
Claraco rather naïvely thought for a while that the missing pesos
were none of his business, while the other two principal treasury
officials in New Providence, who knew some explanation was necessary, made certain that it was. Yturrieta and Cartas returned
to Havana before Claraco, giving them a head start on assigning
blame for the missing money. Since treasury accounts were naturally a hacienda concern, hearings on the case were conducted by

treasury officials, all of whom were acquaintances of their two Bahamian brethren and all of whom were imbued with a deep distrust and dislike for army officers like Claraco. Because the director of the exchequer was the most powerful official in Havana after the war, Claraco's determination to keep his powder dry in Nassau plunged him into legal deep water upon returning from his Bahamian captivity.[39]

For four years the hapless Captain Claraco fought a pesky but losing battle with the exchequer from prison. He did not deny that he had ordered the money box opened. Since the garrison held out for six days against the British, hostile judges rejected Claraco's excuse that the attack was enough of an emergency to override normal treasury procedures. Claraco's witnesses were mainly military men, suspect even before giving testimony in this court. The former governor offered no proof that treasury incompetence or anything else explained the wayward funds.

In 1788 the hacienda court found Claraco responsible for most of the missing money, and it assessed him an additional fine for the amount of treasury funds confiscated as booty by Deveaux after the conquest. The tribunal also decided that the former governor had violated other exchequer regulations. Altogether Claraco was ordered to pay over 1,000 pesos. To assure that the fine was collected, the treasury decided to retain one-half of Claraco's salary. Later on, he was assessed an additional amount for the legal costs of the hearings, a substantial amount considering that scribes and lawyers had worked on the case for four years.[40] Although discouraged at his plight, Claraco still had hope. If he could move his legal battles to a court more sympathetic to his position, he might be able to outflank the treasury.

It was Claraco's good fortune that his arrest upon returning to Havana was performed by the Spanish army. Indeed, Claraco may have intentionally arranged for this to happen. The exchequer proceedings thus had taken place while the former governor was in the custody of his fellow army officers, a group that could empathize with his misfortune. Claraco undoubtedly had more freedom under army scrutiny than he would have had under other circumstances. His major concern while in military custody was to persuade his own branch of the government to give him a hearing. Not until 1791 did the Spanish army convene its own judges, all army officers, to consider Claraco's case. The central question now was whether he had defended Spanish honor before capitulating to Deveaux.

Aside from the notoriously slow pace of eighteenth-century justice there were good reasons for the Spanish army to take eight years to convene a court-martial. Because Claraco was confined in Nassau for sixteen months after the war, most of the witnesses to events in New Providence had departed Havana before the former governor returned. In fact, they were scattered throughout the empire, and it took years to locate many of them. Military prosecutors finally collected testimony from such diverse places as Mexico, Florida, Puerto Rico, the Canary Islands, and Cuba. The former Bahamian governor contributed to the leisurely pace of his ordeal by expending much energy on the exchequer hearings against him in Havana. Internal army politics also delayed bringing Claraco's case to court. Claraco's principal patron had been Juan Manuel de Cagigal, whose own career had been destroyed in part by his split with the powerful Gálvez clan. The most distinguished Spanish general in the immediate postwar years was Bernardo de Gálvez. Bernardo's father, Matías de Gálvez, served as viceroy of Mexico. Bernardo's uncle, José de Gálvez, occupied the post of minister of the Indies until 1787. To be on bad terms with this family meant that Claraco had no means of securing swift justice. Moreover, a court-martial immediately after the war would probably have convicted Claraco, just as the exchequer hearing had.

By the end of the 1780s, however, the obstacles to a military hearing on Claraco's conduct in the Bahamas began to disappear. The Gálvez family barrier vanished through the unexpected deaths of Bernardo, Matías, and José. Their successors had different political agendas. Indifference toward the plight of Claraco also began to dissipate. The number of years that he had remained in custody evoked a certain sympathy among army officers who felt that the captain deserved a decision on his case. The persistence of Claraco also played a role. The former governor never abandoned his efforts to obtain justice. As in his prison days in Nassau, Claraco used his time to bombard superiors with requests for help, hearings, and anything else that could result in his freedom. His efforts finally bore fruit.

In 1789 Charles IV ordered that Claraco be sent to Spain under arrest to face a court-martial. All the information collected in Cuba up to that point was to accompany him.[41] This royal directive further stipulated that all senior officers who had been in the Bahamas when the surrender took place were to be arrested and informed that they would face the same court-martial. Had all defended the army's honor before surrendering? To save money, those officers still physically in the New World, for the most part men still serving with the Corona regiment in Mexico, were to be sent only to Cuba and interrogated in the presence of the former governor before he left for Europe. Those in Spain, officers who had returned to Europe with the España regiment, would stand before the court with Claraco. The former governor's day in court was in sight.

It took nearly a year for Claraco to arrive in Spain. He reached Cádiz in June 1790. Once there, it took nearly another year for the military tribunal to convene in Madrid. In September 1791, over a period of eleven days, Claraco and his fellow officers presented their defense for surrendering New Providence before a tribunal composed of three lieutenant generals (*teniente generales*) and three field marshals (*mariscales del campo*), a high-ranking group of judges. Captain Claraco argued that he had defended Nassau to the best of his ability and held on as long as resources and honor required. If there was any disgrace in the battle for New Providence, it rested with the British, who blatantly violated a signed truce, and not with the Spaniards, who honored it. The court decided by a plurality of votes, not unanimously, that Claraco was innocent of any wrongdoing in the capitulation of the Bahamas and that he was worthy of special compensation for his travails since then.[42] The court recommended that he be given an audience with the king and that he be promoted to lieutenant colonel, receiving seniority dating back to the period when he would have normally reached this rank.

The king accepted these recommendations. Claraco took his new rank immediately, and within a year his regiment promoted him again, this time to the rank of colonel.[43] Equally important for Claraco the court instructed the exchequer in Havana to refund the salary withheld from him during his eight-year ordeal. His fellow officers who had served in New Providence were also exonerated, although those with the España regiment were reprimanded for expressing doubts about the propriety of surrendering during their testimony before the tribunal. Noting that they had signed the capitulation agreement unconditionally, the court felt that any reservations about capitulation were inappropriate so long after the fact. Perhaps Claraco's detractors in the España regiment truly had second thoughts about his leadership in Nassau. It is also possible that they had tried to distance themselves from Claraco in case the court found the former governor guilty.

Claraco had now been exonerated by a second trial long after losing the first. Wise to the ways of Spanish bureaucracy, he cleverly proceeded to use his success before the military tribunal to undo the damage suffered because of the unfavorable judgment in the exchequer court in Havana. Hacienda officials in Cuba argued doggedly that the money withheld in Havana had nothing to do with Claraco's military duties. Instead, his fines stemmed from his incompetence and malfeasance as a treasury official in Nassau. Colonel Claraco, however, secured royal orders instructing the Havana intendant to refund immediately the former governor's salary "without detaining the issue with further queries and interpretations."[44] Notwithstanding this clear directive, the hacienda dragged out compliance by further queries and questions of interpretation.

Eventually the former governor got most of his money back, and he finally freed himself from the Bahamian imbroglio.[45] He was now at liberty to resume his military career, which he did just in time to see action against revolutionary France from 1793 to 1795. In this struggle Claraco found himself once again in a very familiar situation. He was captured by the French and spent several months as a prisoner of war before being exchanged. Few Spanish officers lost more years to one type of confinement or another than did the former governor of the Bahamas. Evidently chastened by his last military experience, Claraco left the army shortly after the French war. Taking advantage of the English he learned while in Nassau, he served for nearly a decade as a vice-consul of the United States in Spain.[46] His life had been forever shaped by his governorship of New Providence.

Chapter Seven

CONCLUSION

The Spanish period in Bahamian history is rarely more than a footnote—if, indeed, even that—in most accounts of the war years from 1775 to 1783. Even scholars who have concentrated their work exclusively on the history of the Bahamas have failed to give this period more than the most cursory glance.[1] Yet the last year of the war and the controversies surrounding New Providence deserve far more attention than they have received. Uniqueness alone makes the history of the colony intriguing. Many Spanish possessions fell under British control during the eighteenth century; only a few British colonies suffered the reverse fate. New Providence was one. However, it is not just the singularity of Spanish domination over a British colony that sets 1782–83 off from other times. The Spanish Bahamas merit scholarly scrutiny because this period affected the future of the newly independent mainland colonies, the Spanish empire, and the Bahamas themselves.

The conquest of the Bahamas represented the apex of American naval accomplishments during the Revolution. No other rebel maritime endeavor came close to matching the achievements of the frigate *South Carolina* and the other American ships under Commodore Gillon. Why this achievement has received so little recognition in American history is an interesting puzzle not to be addressed here. Little did the crew and officers of the *South Carolina* benefit from their labors. Gillon's subsequent career was marked in part by his need to defend himself against numerous claims for debts engendered in outfitting and manning the *South Carolina*. Perhaps the commodore's involvement with radical local politics after the war explains the lethargy with which his home state moved in assuming its responsibility for the financial obligations of its principal ship. Only after the commodore's death in 1794 did South Carolina recognize and accept its financial responsibilities for its wartime navy. By this time, of course, Gillon was no longer alive to assist with a rendering of these obligations.

As important as these debts might have seemed for the moment, the greatest significance of the events in the Bahamas for the fledgling republic was their influence upon subsequent Spanish-American relations. It is ironic that the most important example of cooperation between the armed forces of the rebels and Spain during the war led to hard feelings after the conflict. Yet it did. Bound uneasily together during the war years by a common enemy, Spain and the United States were hardly nations destined to have friendly ties after the war. There were too many points of potential disagreement between the two.

Spanish perception that Cagigal had been deserted by the South Carolina navy at a critical junction in the assault upon New Providence contributed to some of the rougher moments in the relations between the two countries. When worried Spaniards expelled all Americans from Havana in 1784–85 in a last-ditch effort to seal the trading breach that the island's neighbors had opened during the war, Cuban officials carried out the expulsion with unusual rigor and zeal, in part because of the residue of ill will arising from Gillon's conduct a few years before.[2] Indeed, years later, to have been one of the *South Carolina*'s crew was reason enough to arouse Spanish suspicion. In the 1780s Juan Manuel de Zéspedes, governor of East Florida after its return to Spanish control, disparagingly described James O'Fallon, surgeon aboard the *South Carolina* for part of her voyage, as obviously untrustworthy, as would be anyone who had shipped with Gillon.[3]

Spain too felt the impact of its time in New Providence. Some military careers floundered and sank in the waters of the Bahamas. Antonio Claraco y Sanz, the most important of the Spanish governors, gained a decade-long imprisonment and trial for his labor in governing and defending this Spanish possession. First in Nassau, then in Havana, and finally in Cádiz and Madrid, Claraco tenaciously fought to free himself from the legal entanglements which had blighted his professional life. Juan Manuel de Cagigal, by far the highest ranking Spanish officer to be tainted by the Bahamian episode, found that the rewards for his victory of May 1782 were negligible. Indeed, his future as a military officer might have been better served had he never organized and led the expedition against New Providence. Much like Claraco, Cagigal spent the better part of a decade after the war justifying his success at Nassau and other aspects of his term as captain general of Havana.

In the long run the greatest legacy of the Spanish conquest of the Bahamas was its effect upon the life of Francisco de Miranda. Miranda was already in trouble with superiors in Spain for his activities while stationed in Havana; his last realistic hope for a successful career in the Spanish military rested with the honors that should have accrued to a key figure in the conquest of the Bahamas. When the expected rewards failed to materialize, Miranda lacked the patience, resources, and confidence to take his chances with army justice, as Cagigal and Claraco did. Surely his later adventures as a leading figure in the fight for Latin American independence owed something, probably a great deal, to the setback his career had suffered as a result of the New Providence expedition.[4]

Personal tragedies and triumphs aside, this brief period of Spanish rule in the Bahamas left a mark upon Spanish history in other ways. The capture of a foreign colony in 1782 presented Spanish officials with an opportunity to establish a local government that incorporated the most recent political changes and reforms at home and in the empire. It would be an exaggeration to maintain that New Providence was completely a governmental tabula rasa for the Spaniards, presenting no limitations on the type and style of rule they could impose. The capitulation accords signed by Cagigal and Maxwell left a considerable part of the British colonial system intact to function as it always had. Ultimately the Spanish administrators of the island governed in ways closer to the British model of colonial rule than to the Hispanic prototype.[5] There was considerable opportunity for the best of eighteenth-century political practices to be instituted in Nassau, but the opposite happened.

In many ways it was the darker side of Spanish government which flourished in Nassau. The New Providence experience did little, for example, to heal the serious breach between the Spanish army and navy. In fact it magnified this unfortunate quarrel. Throughout the Spanish occupation of the Bahamas the Spanish navy operated as if it had no responsibility for the defense of that colony. Without adequate naval protection New Providence was vulnerable to successful attack by very modest forces. This is precisely what happened in April 1783 with the assault by Andrew Deveaux and his followers. At the same time, Spanish officials in the Bahamas failed to close the dangerous rift between the royal exchequer and colonial administrators. This chasm was so deep that it could not be forgotten even under the most threatening circumstances, such as an invasion of the island by enemy forces. What made the Spanish government in Nassau so prone to internal squabbles was that it reflected the turmoil brewing in Cuba. In Havana, however, there were experienced officials and administrative procedures to curb contentious bureaucrats. In New Providence there were few veteran officials and no inherent restraints.

While the Spanish experienced some bitter aftereffects of their conquest, it was the Bahamians themselves who were obviously most touched by the foreign invasion, occupation, and expulsion. The four invasions of the colony from 1776 to 1783—particularly the Spanish assault in 1782—drove home to the British crown how defenseless its outpost was. England had defended the colony lightly, hoping rather than ensuring that it would not be attacked. This policy was scarcely reassuring to the inhabitants of the islands, who lived so close to major Spanish and French military bases. Subsequently the home government made a concerted effort to improve the defenses of the islands.[6] And, in fact, never again did an enemy force storm the colony's forts. Yet military events were hardly the most significant aspect of the Spanish occupation for the Bahamas. The Spaniards changed the financial and political history of the colony.

Spanish rule fell heavily upon certain segments of Bahamian society, most notably upon island merchants connected with corsair cruising. As severely as some of these entrepreneurs were punished for their choice of livelihoods, there is no evidence that any were permanently impoverished by the war. Nevertheless, some were certainly damaged and weakened financially. John Miller, for example, was still struggling to pay off wartime loans in 1789, five years after the Union Jack returned to New Providence.[7] Moreover, the temporary reverses inflicted upon some of these key Nassau businessmen made them much less able to meet the challenges of outside merchants who settled in the Bahamas after the war. Certainly local entrepreneurs might have mounted a more effective effort to monopolize the lucrative Indian trade in the Floridas after the war had their finances been more secure.[8]

While financial gains and losses were affected by the occupation, there is no question that the most significant aspect of the Spanish period for Bahamian history was the timing of the return to British rule. With the American Revolution having taken a bitter and disastrous turn for the most militant of the loyalists, there were thousands of political refugees in the early months of 1783 looking for a safe haven. For most of these individuals there was no possibility of an early return home. Although some exiles from the mainland struggles ventured to the Bahamas while the colony was still Spanish, few would risk such a move while the islands were in enemy hands. The negative and exaggerated publicity over the Spanish crackdown on the *armadores* made the Bahamas extremely unattractive to men of property.[9] Nor could or would most of these exiles have waited patiently in Florida and New York for the leisurely procedures of international diplomacy to have returned suzerainty over New Providence to Great Britain. Few had the personal resources to wait indefinitely before earning a livelihood again. With the sudden and unexpected return of British rule in April, 1783, the most mobile of the loyalist community now had an immediate and nearby sanctuary. Many took advantage of the Bahamian opportunity.

Equally important for later events, these new residents in the Bahamas encountered a weak provisional government. Andrew Deveaux, leader of the reconquest, was not an islander and had little intention of settling down. When he did finally plant roots, it was in New York and not in New Providence. He left behind an ad hoc administration which marked time until the crown could send a royal governor. When one did appear, it turned out to be John Maxwell, a timid individual already disgraced locally for being the person who had surrendered the colony to the Spaniards in 1782. Because of the circumstances of his first departure Maxwell was a governor with limited prestige and authority.

The new settlers were hardly republicans, yet neither were they docile monarchists. They were well familiar with local governments in turmoil and chaos. Most had been profoundly changed by their long struggles on the mainland, and they had strong views on their rights as Englishmen. Many were accustomed to exercising power and authority, and most expected a considerable voice in the island government, particularly in a colonial government not noted for its impassioned loyalty to the crown. To the dismay of longtime inhabitants of New Providence, loyalist newcomers fought hard, skillfully, and relentlessly to gain political control over their new homeland.[10] By 1784 island politics had degenerated into a three-way contest among new settlers, old residents, and the royal governor. In some ways New Providence was more open politically than the former mainland colonies which composed the new Confederation. There, one large segment of public opinion, the loyalist, had been discredited and silenced. A much more active electorate meant that the old governing patterns of antebellum Nassau were gone forever.

Although limited in time to less than a year, the Spanish period in Bahamian history thus influenced later affairs significantly. Perhaps more than anything, close scrutiny of the final year of the war shows that not all important action during the American Revolution took place within the confines of the rebellious Thirteen Colonies. Certainly New Providence experienced more invasions, more shifts in control, and more internal upheavals in 1782 and 1783 than did most areas in the entire war. In the end, the Spanish Bahamas played a much more complex and interesting part in the general history of the war than scholars have traditionally recognized.

ABBREVIATIONS

AA—Audited Accounts, Columbia, SC
AGI—Archivo General de Indias, Seville
AGMS—Archivo General Militar de Segovia
AGS—Archivo General de Simancas
AHN—Archivo Histórico Nacional, Madrid
AO—Audit Office, London
BPRO—Bahamas Public Record Office, Nassau
CO—Colonial Office, London
CS—Consejos Suprimidos, Madrid
DLDS—Domestic Letters of the Department of State, Washington
exp.—Expediente (bundle)
FO—Foreign Office, London
f., fs.—Foja, Fojas (page, pages)
GAP—General Assembly Papers, Columbia, SC
GM—Guerra Moderna, Simancas
i—Item
IG—Indiferente General, Seville
Leg.—Legajo (volume)
M—Microfilm Publication of NARS
MPCC—Miscellaneous Papers of the Continental Congress, Washington
n.—Note
NARS—National Archives and Records Service of the United States, Washington

Num.—Numero (number)
PCC—Papers of the Continental Congress, Washington
PRO—Public Record Office, London
PRO 30/55—Carleton Papers, London
pza.—Pieza (section)
r—Reel Number
RG—Record group, Washington
RWP—Revolutionary War Pension and Bounty-Land-Warrant Application Files, Washington
SCSA—South Carolina State Archives, Columbia
SD—Santo Domingo, Seville
v.—Verso

NOTES

CHAPTER 1

1. A standard account of the siege of Gibraltar in English is T. H. McGuffie, *The Siege of Gibraltar: 1779–1783*.

2. Recent works such as Mario Rodríguez, *La Revolución Americana de 1776 y el Mundo Hispánico: Ensayos y Documentos*, should be compared with pioneering studies by Manuel Conrotte, *La Intervención de España en la Independencia de los Estados Unidos de la América del Norte*, and Juan F. Yela Utrilla, *España ante la Independencia de los Estados Unidos*.

3. As important as José de Gálvez was in Spanish history, it is remarkable that he has never received a full-length biography. For an outline of his life see Mark A. Burkholder, *Biographical Dictionary of Councilors of the Indies, 1717–1808*.

4. Students of Bourbon Spain will recognize all four of these names. Most have received some biographical attention. For Gálvez, see John Walton Caughey, *Bernardo de Gálvez in Louisiana, 1776–1783*. Cagigal awaits a biographer. Solano has received kind treatment in José Luis Santaló Rodríguez de Viguri, *Don José Solano y Bote: Primer Marqués del Socorro, Capitán General de la Armada*. Information on Saavedra can be found in James A. Lewis, "Las Damas de la Havana, El Precursor, and Francisco de Saavedra: A Note on Spanish Participation in the Battle of Yorktown"; Manuel Ignacio Pérez Alonso, S.J., ed. and trans., "War Mission in the Caribbean: The Diary of Don Francisco de Saavedra (1780–1783)"; and Angel López Canto, *Don Francisco de Saavedra, Segundo Intendente de Caracas*.

5. Lillian Estelle Fisher, *The Last Inca Revolt, 1780–1783*; John Leddy Phelan, *The People and the King: The Comunero Revolution in Colombia, 1781*; James A. Lewis, "New Spain during the American Revolution, 1779–1783: A Viceroyalty at War," 238–48.

6. The Florida campaign can be followed in Francisco de Borja Medina Rojas,

José de Ezpeleta: Gobernador de la Mobila, 1780–1781; Caughey, *Gálvez in Louisiana*, 187–214; and William S. Coker and Hazel P. Coker, *The Siege of Pensacola in Maps*.

7. Lewis, "Las Damas," 83–99. Guillermo Porras Muñoz, "El Fracaso de Guarico."

8. AGI, IG 1584, reserved letter 20, B. Gálvez to Solano, Havana, 3 Jan. 1782.

9. Huet's disappointment was no secret. See AGI, Cuba 224–A, reserved letter 50, B. Gálvez to J. Gálvez, Guarico, 5 Aug. 1782.

10. These five Cagigals were (1) el Marqués de Cagigal, (2) Gaspar de Cagigal, (3) Francisco de Cagigal, (4) el Marqués de Casa Cagigal, and (5) Juan Manuel de Cagigal. AHN, Estado 3152[1], exp. 8, Memorial from Cagigal, Madrid, 26 Mar. 1793. For Cagigal's version of his contribution at Pensacola, see AHN, CS 20170, exp. 4, pza. 3, pp. 31–70, Cagigal's apology, Madrid, 14 Apr. 1790.

11. AGI, IG 1584, Cagigal to B. Gálvez, Havana, 20 Jan. 1782.

12. These rather unfortunate events can be followed in a number of sources. Joshua Barney, an American sea captain whose ship was commandeered for the African campaign, left a graphic description. See Mary Barney, *Biographical Memoir of the Late Commodore Joshua Barney*, 24. Cagigal himself expressed the army's view of the navy at Gibraltar and on convoy duty between Spain and the New World. See AHN, CS 20170, exp. 4, pza. 3, pp. 31–70, Cagigal's apology, Madrid, 14 Apr. 1790. For the famous dispute at Pensacola, see Eric Beerman, "José de Solano and the Spanish Navy at the Siege of Pensacola"; and Jack D. L. Holmes, "Bernardo de Gálvez: Spain's 'Man of the Hour' During the Revolution," 169–70.

13. The French view is best seen in Harold A. Larrabee, *Decision at the Chesapeake* 146; and "A Neglected French Collaborator in the Victory at Yorktown: Claude-Anne Marquis de Saint-Simon (1740–1819)." For an idea of French influence in the ministry of the Indies see James A. Lewis, "The Royal Gunpowder Monopoly in New Spain (1766–1783): A Case Study of Management, Technology, and Reform under Charles III."

14. Upon leaving Texel the *South Carolina* carried 557 men (315 marines and 242 sailors). Her dimensions included a keel of 168 feet, a beam of 47 feet, a main mast of 103 feet, and a draught of 22 feet. She mounted 28 cannon on the main deck (all 36 pounders) and 12 on the quarter deck and forecastle (all long 12s). Although some secondary sources credit the frigate with more and larger armament, this is due to the confusing nature of eighteenth-century arms. Standardized sizes did not exist across nor occasionally within national borders. The *South Carolina*'s 36 pounders were French made, the equal of British 42 pounders. Her 12 pounders were Dutch designed, the equivalent of British 14 pounders. See John Joyner et al., "Letter to Gillon," Philadelphia, 10 July 1782, *Maryland Journal and Baltimore Advertiser*, 27 Aug. 1782; NARS, RWP, M804, r980, Declaration of George Fisher, Barnwell District, 20 Oct. 1833, pp. 22–28; NARS, DLDS, M40, r3, List of the Fleet, pp. 48–53; Gillon to Col. John Laurens, Amsterdam, 22 Mar. 1781, in D. E. Huger Smith, ed., "The Mission of Col. John Laurens to Europe in 1781," 29; "Account of the Large Rebel Frigate Named the South Carolina, from the Laying of Her Keel until Her Capture," 439.

15. The standard accounts of the *South Carolina* and Gillon are now dated but still useful. See D. E. Huger Smith, "Commodore Alexander Gillon and the

Frigate *South Carolina*"; Louis F. Middlebrook, *The Frigate South Carolina*; and Berkeley Grimball, "Commodore Alexander Gillon of South Carolina, 1741–1794." Although accessible to specialists, the Grimball work merits publication so that a larger audience could have access to its very valuable information.

16. Family information about Gillon can be gleaned from NARS, RWP, M804, r1075, Declaration of Mary S. Brisbane, Litchfield, 14 Jan. 1850, pp. 1000–01; and Grimball, "Commodore Gillon," 1–13.

17. One fiery New World republican not impressed with Gillon's uniform was John Trumbull, the painter. See "Letter from John Trumbull to Jonathan Trumbull," Bilbao, 11 Oct. 1781, "Letters of John Trumbull," 286.

18. Terms of the contract are printed in Middlebrook, *Frigate South Carolina*, 3–4. At least one reference calls the *South Carolina* by the name *Charlestown* or *Union*; see "Account of the Large Rebel Frigate," 438. For a different view of how Gillon received the frigate, see John Paul Jones, *Charges and Proofs Respecting the Conduct of Peter Landais*, 12.

19. No complete list of officers and sailors exists for the *South Carolina*. There are numerous reasons for this. Gillon maintained records in a very haphazard manner. Part of the records that he did keep were utilized for claims against the state long after the war and then misplaced. South Carolina state records suffered severely during the Civil War, eliminating still more of the frigate's written past. Lastly, the crew which manned the frigate was in constant flux. Nevertheless, the names of most of the final crew can be found in Middlebrook, *Frigate South Carolina*, 18–25. Part of the earlier complement of the ship can be pulled out of Bobby Gilmer Moss, *Roster of South Carolina Patriots in the American Revolution*. Useful for names absent from the Moss book is the National Genealogical Society, *Index of Revolutionary War Pension Applications in the National Archives*. For a list of officers see NARS, RWP, M804, r1661, Declaration of John Mayrant, Fairfield District, 14 July 1832, pp. 366–7(; NARS, RWP, M804, r594, Declaration of Alexander Coffin, New York, 20 Apr. 1833, pp. 440–43; NARS, RWP, M804, r2478, Declaration of Richard Briggs, Hampshire County, 11 Sept. 1832, pp. 124–25.

20. The prince of Luxembourg had troops involved in three major campaigns during the war. One group participated in the struggle for India. Another helped with the French invasion of the island of Jersey off the coast of France. The last contingent served on the *South Carolina*. It is likely that most of the marines on the *South Carolina* also took part in the Jersey invasion. Much remains to be learned about these marines. For a start, see D. E. Huger Smith, "The Luxembourg Claims"; NARS, RWP, M804, r2478, Declaration of Richard Briggs, Hampshire County, 11 Sept. 1832, pp. 124–25; SCSA, GAP, 0010/003/ND00/00537/00, Leroy Berthier Deutheraus aux Estatae de la Carolina, n.d.; and *Facts and Observations Justifying the Claims of the Prince of Luxembourg against the State of South Carolina and against Alexander Gillon, Esq., Late Commodore of the Navy of the Said State*, 12–28.

21. Since it was Gillon's personal enemies who emphasized his indebtedness, the commodore's penury might not have been as desperate as portrayed in the paragraph. Yet it most certainly existed. Trumbull to Trumbull, 286–87. "Letter to Gillon," *Maryland Journal*, 27 Aug. 1782. Smith, "Luxembourg Claims," 111–12. "William Jackson to John Adams," Bilbao, 26 Oct. 1781, in L. H. Butterfield and Marc Friedlaender, eds. *Adams Family Correspondence*, 4:235–37. NARS, MPCC,

M332, r4, John de Neufville to Samuel Huntingdon, Amsterdam, 28 Sept. 1781, pp. 604–11.

22. For all of the *South Carolina*'s impressive armament and sleek lines, she turned out to be rather slow in a chase. The first boat that the *South Carolina* took turned out to be worthless and was burned at sea. The second, however, was the *Alexander*, a 16-gun (70–80-man crew) privateer brig, captured off Ireland. This prize was sent to France, just as the Luxembourg contract stipulated, and its crew was added to Gillon's. Before it reached France, however, a British man-of-war retook the *Alexander* and carried her into Liverpool. Only one other boat was taken on the European side of the Atlantic, the brig *Venus*, loaded with codfish. The *South Carolina* towed this boat into Tenerife. NARS, RWP, M804, r594, Declaration of Alexander Coffin, New York, 20 Apr. 1833, pp. 440–43. NARS, RWP, M804, r980, Declaration of George Fisher, Barnwell District, 20 Oct. 1833. NARS,RG 45, Log-Book of the Frigate *South Carolina*, 4 Aug. 1781, to 21 May 1782. "Account of the Large Rebel Frigate," 439.

23. NARS, RG 45, Log-Book; SCSA, AA 3031A, Memorial of Richard Graham, Charleston, 3 Nov. 1803, pp. 584–85.

24. Gillon's duel was reportedly with Major William Jackson. Jackson, Barney, Searle, Trumbull, and Adams (then just a child) left the *South Carolina* at Corunna. Since the only source for the purported duel was Abigail Adams, who lived an ocean away from the event, it must be taken more as a manifestation of hard feelings between some of the passengers and Gillon than as necessarily a verifiable event. For Trumbull, leaving the commodore resulted in one of his extant paintings—*View Toward the Bar of Bilbao*. See "Abigail Adams to John Thaxter," 18 July 1782, in Butterfield and Friedlaender, *Adams Correspondence*, 4:349, and Silas Deane to Isaac Hazelhurst, Ghent, 26 Oct. 1781, *The Deane Papers*, 22:520–21

25. For a critical view of Gillon's enlistment activities see AHN, Estado 3884bis, exp. 16, letter 1, Pedro Martín Cermeño to Miguel de Múzquiz, Corunna, 2 Sept. 1782. AHN, Estado 3884bis, exp. 16, letter 6, John Jay to Gillon, Madrid, 9 Oct. 1781. Jones's view of Gillon's recruitment practices is best seen in the worshipful biography of the admiral by Samuel Eliot Morison, *John Paul Jones: A Sailor's Biography*, 294, 301.

26. Aileen Moore Topping, "Alexander Gillon in Havana, 'This Very Friendly Port.'"

27. AGS, Estado 4628, letter 15, Pedro Lecent to Marqués de la Cañada, Santa Cruz de Tenerife, 27 Nov. 1781; AGS, Estado 4628, letter 18, Cañada to Conde de Floridablanca, Santa Cruz, 26 Dec. 1781.

28. On the *South Carolina*'s approach to Charleston's harbor, the frigate fell in with a British cargo fleet and would have had even more prizes had not bad luck and some poor sailing prevented it. The best accounts of the Jamaica captures are Alexander Garden, *Anecdotes of the American Revolution, Illustrative of the Talents and Virtues of the Heroes and Patriots, Who Acted the Most Conspicuous Parts Therein*, 96–99; and NARS, RWP, M804, r594, Declaration of Alexander Coffin, New York, 20 Apr. 1833, pp. 440–43. For the names and cargoes of the prizes, see AGI, Cuba 1340, attachment to letter 28, Cuenta exacta de la cargazada, Havana, [Feb.

1782]; and NARS, PCC, M247, r73, i59, Memorial from Chevalier de la Luzerne, Philadelphia, 10 Dec. 1782, pp. 159–82.

CHAPTER 2

1. AGI, IG 1584, reserved letter 9, Solano to B. Gálvez, Havana, 11 Nov. 1781. NARS, DLDS, M40, r3, pp. 2–7, Gillon to William Moultrie, Ashley Hill, 28 June 1786. AGI, SD 1234, reserved letter 25, Cagigal to J. Gálvez, Havana, 23 Jan. 1782. Pérez Alonso, "War Mission," 4:394–95.

2. Pérez Alonso, "War Mission," 4:395.

3. By the time the Gálvez cancellation order reached Havana, however, the New Providence convoy had sailed. AGI, IG 1584, reserved letter 16, B. Gálvez to Cagigal, Guarico, 12 Apr. 1782.

4. The Havana exchequer contracted to pay foreign privateers a monthly rate based on tonnage (ten and a half pesos per ton), starting with the sailing date of the expedition and running through a week after its conclusion. The exchequer further insured the American vessels against loss of their ships and cargoes during the campaign. See AGI, IG 1579, exp. 11, José Ignacio de Urriza to B. Gálvez, Havana, 29 Apr. 1782; AGI, Cuba 1308, letter 625, Urriza to Cagigal, Havana, 17 Dec. 1782. Just how effective the shipping embargo in Havana was can be seen from the port records called *Entradas y Salidas*. From January to May 1782 nearly 90 foreign ships entered the harbor of Havana but only 31 departed. Half of those departures were American vessels sailing with the New Providence expedition. Almost all the rest left on official, rather than private, business. See AGI, Cuba 1331, SD 1235, and IG 2421, Relaciones de Entradas y Salidas, [Havana, Jan.–May 1782]; also AGI, Cuba 1311, letter 17, Order of Commandant of Morro Castle, Havana, 12 Feb. 1782.

5. The two major convoys for the Cape left Havana on 5 March (78 ships) and 14 April (21 ships). See Relaciones de Entradas y Salidas in n. 4.

6. NARS, DLDS, M40, r3, pp. 11–13, Gillon to Cagigal, on board the *South Carolina*, Havana, 19 Apr. 1782. SCSA, AA 118, Memorial of William Pickett, Charleston, 24 Feb. 1796. SCSA, Commodore's Ledger, 1779–84, Gillon, p. 107b. AGI, IG 1580, exp. 31, Summary of Alexander Deker, Havana, 3 Apr. 1782. AGI, IG 1580, Testimony of Pablo Renard, Frigate *Nuestra Señora de la O*, 14 Apr. 1782. AGI, Cuba 1318, letter 12, Gillon to Cagigal, Havana, 18 Mar. 1782. AGI, Cuba 1318, attachment to letter 9, List of Deserters [Gillon], Havana, Feb. 1782.

7. The exact size of the convoy and the total number of American ships are not easy to determine, particularly since those on the scene counted differently. The *South Carolina*, to illustrate one problem, sailed with her own tender, a schooner called *The Surprise*. Some counted both vessels as one ship, others listed them separately. Also complicating the count was the tendency of ships to join or leave the venture at any time. Even once at sea the number grew when Gillon forced several Spanish truce ships to sail with the convoy. There were also prizes taken along the way. Gillon's count, which should have been reasonably accurate since it was his responsibility to know where each member of the convoy was, gave 59 ships

(13 American) in one document and 62 vessels (16 foreign) in another. Intendant Urriza, who had to pay for each ship, reported 57 ships (12 American). NARS, DLDS, M40, r3, pp. 48–53, 68–69, List of the Fleet and the Form of the Fleets Sailing . . . against the Bahama Islands. AGI, IG 1579, exp. 11, Urriza to B. Gálvez, Havana, 29 Apr. 1782. For other counts, all very close to the above, see AGI, IG 2421, Relaciones de Entradas y Salidas, [Havana, Apr. 1782]; AGS, Estado 8143, note M, *Suplement aux Affiches Américaines*, 24 July 1782; and AGI, IG 1583, Cagigal to B. Gálvez, New Providence, 20 May 1782. A recent popular account of the expedition put the total at 62 (8 American); see Eric Beerman, "The 1782 American-Spanish Expedition," 87.

8. Spanish units in the expedition were the following:

Unit Name	Soldiers
Regiment of Guadalajara	668
Regiment of España	594
Regiment of Corona of New Spain	326
Artillery Units and Support Staff	140
Light Infantry	50
Pardo and Moreno Companies	202
	1980

Sources: AGI, IG 1583, Estado [de] la expedición del Cagigal, Juan Nepomuceno de Quesada, Havana, 8 Apr. 1782; NARS, DLDS, M40, r3, pp. 48–53, List of the Fleet; Allan J. Kuethe, *Cuba, 1753–1815: Crown, Military, and Society,* 117–18. In no case did the Spaniards commit an entire regiment to the expedition. Guadalajara and España were at battalion strength, Corona and the rest at several companies or less.

9. Three of the pilots were William Woodsides, Downham Newton, and William (Jeremiah?) Newton—the latter two brothers. Some historians have asserted that all three were natives of Charleston who lived in Philadelphia during the war. British officials maintained that the Newtons, at least, were Bahamians. Like many men of the sea, it was possible that they had several residencies. Governor Maxwell complained bitterly that the Spanish fleet had been brought to his door by traitors. Smith, "Alexander Gillon," 215. John Maxwell to Lord George Germain, New Providence, 14 May 1782, in John Almon, ed., *The Remembrance,* 2:148–49. PRO, CO 26/10/1–3, General Assembly, 20 Apr. 1784. *The Royal Gazette* (Charleston), 1–5 June 1782. PRO, CO23/10/242v–43, Minutes of Council, 17 Feb. 1776. PRO, CO23/10/273–73v, Certification of John Pratt, Bahama Islands, 13 Mar. 1780. P.C. Coker, III, *Charleston's Maritime Heritage, 1670–1865,* 88, 300.

10. There is some controversy over the precise route that the convoy took to New Providence. At various times both Cagigal and Gillon claimed separately to have discovered a new approach to Nassau. Gillon certainly had two earlier experiences at traveling through or past the Bahamas (1778 and 1781). Because of the substantial draught of the *South Carolina,* so deep that she had to be hulled over on her side for some 70 miles when moving from Amsterdam to the coast, the fleet must have stayed close to the deep channels of the traditional routes from Havana to Nassau. NARS, PCC, M247, r86, pp. 143–50, Gillon to Mathews, on board the *South Carolina,* 15 May 1782. AGI, SD 2085–B, letter 133, Cagigal to

B. Gálvez, New Providence, 20 May 1782. AHN, CS 20170, exp. 4, pza. 1, pp. 83–99, Memorandum of Cagigal, Cádiz, 18 July 1786. Gillon to Henry Laurens, Havana, 18 Sept. 1778, "Letters from Commodore Gillon in 1778 and 1779," 75–76. AGI, SD 1234, reserved letter 25, Cagigal to B. Gálvez, Havana, 21 Apr. 1782. "Account of the Large Rebel Frigate," 438.

11. NARS, DLDS, M40, r3, pp. 54–60, Gillon to Cagigal, on board the *South Carolina*, 6 May 1782. A Spanish copy of this letter is dated 8 May; see AHN, CS 20170, exp. 4, pza. 2, pp. 1–5v.

12. NARS, DLDS, M40, r3, pp. 2–7, Gillon to Moultrie, Ashley Hill, 28 June 1786.

13. Although a number of people commented on this dispute, the most detailed account of the affair came from Juan Martín Galiano, an exchequer official who accompanied the expedition. AGI, SD 2084, letter 965, attachments 1 and 3, Galiano to J. Gálvez and Urriza, New Providence, 23 and 15 May 1782.

14. Indeed, the intendant of the exchequer in Havana maintained that Gillon escorted the convoy with no expectation of compensation whatsoever. Without questioning the sincerity of this statement, such a selfless gesture would not have been typical of the commodore's character or situation. AGI, Cuba 1340, letter 28, Urriza to Luis de Unzaga, Havana, 1 Feb. 1783. AGI, SD 2085–B, letter 133, attachment 2, Cagigal to B. Gálvez, New Providence, 20 May 1783. Also n. 13.

15. AGI, IG 1581, O'Kenny (O'Kelly?) to Geronimo Giron, New Providence, 23 May 1782.

16. In the long and complicated court-martial against Cagigal after the war (AHN, CS 20170), the former captain general never once repudiated his former aide-de-camp, a man who by then had considerable notoriety. In one of those frequent ironies of history Cagigal's namesake and cousin spent much of his career after the turn of the century suppressing unrest in Venezuela, unrest whose roots Miranda had something to do with. See Salvador de Madariaga, *Bolívar*, 135.

17. Gillon to Miranda, Havana, 9 Apr. 1782, *Archivo del General Miranda*, 5:191–92.

18. Cagigal to Gillon, Nassau, 13 May 1782, in *Archivo Miranda*, 5:194–95.

19. Francisco de Miranda, *The New Democracy in America: Travels of Francisco de Miranda in the United States, 1783–1784*, 31. NARS, DLDS, M40, r3, pp. 2–7, Gillon to Moultrie, Ashley Hill, 28 June 1786. AHN, CS 20170, exp. 4, pza. 1, pp. 47–50, 83–99, Declarations of Cagigal, Cádiz, 8 June 1785 and 12 July 1786.

20. Gillon later insisted that he never approved the surrender accords and thus refused to sign them. It is evident from Spanish documentation that the commodore was not presented with an option to sign the capitulation agreement. The Spanish foreign office, however, shortly thereafter apologized to American representatives about the initial willingness of Cagigal to send the captured British garrison to a mainland port, claiming that Cagigal and Bernardo de Gálvez had not received general instructions sent to all Indies officials forbidding such arrangements. NARS, PCC, M247, r86, i72, pp. 143–50, Gillon to Mathews, on board the *South Carolina*, 15 May 1782. NARS, PCC, M247, r116, i88, pp. 253–58, William Carmichael to Robert Livingston, St. Ildefonso, 8 Sept. 1782.

21. NARS, DLDS, M40, r3, pp. 2–7, Gillon to Moultrie, Ashley Hill, 28 June 1786.

22. Maxwell to Lt. Gen. Leslie, Bahamas, 6 May 1782, in Almon, *Remembrancer*, 2: 149. PRO, CO23/25/48–48v, Maxwell to Germain, New Providence, 14 May 1782. PRO, CO26/6/257v, Declaration of Benjamin Watkins, New Providence, 20 Mar. 1780. PRO, CO37/22/134–35v, Pat Tonyn to Maxwell, St. Augustine, 30 June 1781. *The Pennsylvania Packet*, 6 June 1782.

23. PRO, CO37/22/128–29, Maxwell to Lords Commissioners, New Providence, 16 Mar. 1781.

24. Michael Craton, *A History of the Bahamas*, 156–57. PRO, CO23/9/93, Proclamation of Montfort Browne, New Providence, 4 Jan. 1779. PRO, CO23/10/81–3, Browne to Germain, Nassau, 24 Sept. 1779. BPRO, Council Minutes, Nassau, ll Apr. 1780, pp. 637–40.

25. PRO, CO23/10/119, Resolution of Council, New Providence, 3 Apr. 1780.

26. PRO, CO23/24/197–97v, Browne to Capt. Terril, Government House, 26 May 1779. PRO, CO23/24/393, Maxwell to Germain, New Providence, 24 June 1780. PRO, CO23/25/1–1v, Maxwell to Germain, New Providence, 14 Sept. 1780.

27. Miranda reported that Maxwell's forces numbered 274 soldiers, 338 militia, and 800 sailors—some 1,412 men altogether. Cagigal's army was composed of approximately 2,000 regulars and militia. Governor Maxwell claimed 170 men. Statistical disputes were not uncommon in eighteenth century warfare. In this case Miranda was closer to the truth if the total number of potential soldiers was counted, while Maxwell would be correct if the discussion centered around those most likely to fight. AGS, Estado 8143, note M, *Suplement aux Affiches Américaines*, 24 July 1782. Maxwell to Thomas Townsend, New Providence, 14 May 1782, in Almon, *Remembrancer*, 2:148.

28. Maxwell to Germain, New Providence, 14 May 1782, in Almon, *Remembrancer*, 2: 148–49.

29. Cagigal to Maxwell, New Providence, 6 May 1782 and Maxwell to Cagigal, New Providence, 7 May 1782, *Archivo Miranda*, 5:125–26. AGI, SD 2084, letter 965, Urriza to J. Gálvez, Havana, 10 June 1782.

30. AGI, SD 1234, Cagigal to B. Gálvez, Havana, 14 Mar. 1782.

CHAPTER 3

1. Smith, "Alexander Gillon," p. 215.

2. *Pennsylvania Packet*, 30 May 1782.

3. E. James Ferguson, ed., *The Papers of Robert Morris, 1781–1784*, 5:106.

4. For a taste of the Searle-Jackson assault on Gillon, see John Joyner et al. to Gillon, Philadelphia, 10 July 1782, *The Maryland Journal and Baltimore Advertiser*, 27 Aug. 1782. Also Ferguson, *Papers of Morris*, 4:393–94; 7:22.

5. Ferguson, *Papers of Morris*, 6:397.

6. The subsequent fate of the American frigate is unknown, but the ship's bell ended up in India, where it was still being used at a jute mill near Calcutta

as late as 1945. See Richard G. Stone, "'The *South Carolina* We've Lost': The Bizarre Saga of Alexander Gillon and His Frigate"; Middlebrook, *Frigate South Carolina*, 16–17; Norman M. Smith to Admiral Randall Jacobs, Columbia, 11 May 1945, NARS, RG 45, Introduction to the Log-Book of the *South Carolina*.

7. For a summary of Miranda's troubles see William S. Robertson, *The Life of Miranda*, 1:21–34; J. H. Parry, "Eliphalet Fitch: A Yankee Trader in Jamaica during the War of Independence"; and AHN, CS 20878, pza. 23, Estado de los autos sobre Dn. Francisco de Miranda, D. Verdue, Madrid, 20 Sept. 1799.

8. Lt. Gen. [sic] John Campbell to B. Gálvez, New York, 17 July 1782, in Historical Manuscripts Commission, *Report on American Manuscripts in the Royal Institutions of Great Britain*, 3:22–23. Bernardo de Gálvez also had a dispute with another member of this clan, Captain James Campbell, who was a staff officer at Pensacola. Gilberto Antonio de Saint Maxent, who was Gálvez's father-in-law, would personally suffer for these perceived abuses when fate brought him to Jamaica during the war and placed him under the control of yet a third member of the Scottish family, Governor Archibald Campbell. See PRO, CO137/30/71–2, Archibald Campbell to Lord North, Jamaica, Jan. 1784.

9. J. Gálvez to Cagigal, San Lorenzo, 2 Nov. 1781, *Archivo Miranda*, 5:79.

10. AGS, Estado 8143, note M, *Suplement aux Affiches Américaines*, 24 July 1782. AGS, Estado 8141, exp. 7, Miranda to Floridablanca, London, 10 Apr. 1785.

11. [Francisco de Miranda?], "A Particular and Just Account of the Taking of Providence Extracted from a French Paper," *The Maryland Journal and Baltimore Advertiser*, 15 Oct. 1782. Robert Smith to Miranda, Cape François, 6 Dec. 1782, in *Archivo Miranda*, 5:234.

12. Miranda to Cagigal, Cape François, 22 June 1782, *Archivo Miranda*, 5:130.

13. AGI, SD 1234, letter 249, Decision of the Junta, Juan Dabán et al., Havana, 25 May 1782.

14. Cagigal himself inadvertently encouraged rumors that the rest of the convoy had been attacked by corsairs when he asked for naval protection for the ships that had yet to arrive. See AGI, Cuba 1309, letter 161, attachment 1, Cagigal to Juan José de Salaverría, Havana, 21 June 1782; AGI, IG 1583, letter 75, Cagigal to B. Gálvez, Havana, 4 June 1782; AGI, IG 2421, Cuba 1332, Entradas y Salidas, Havana, [May–June, 1782]; AGI, Estado 6–1, Mannrique to Antonio Claraco y Sanz, New Providence, 1 July 1782; AGI, Cuba 1311, letter 48, Mannrique to Cagigal, aboard the frigate *San Luciano*, 3 June 1782.

15. AHN, CS 20170, exp. 4, pza. 1, Solano to González de Castejón, Havana, 26 July 1782. AHN, CS 20170, exp. 4, pza. 3, pp. 31–70, Cagigal's apology, Madrid, 14 Apr. 1790. AGI, SD 2085–B, letter 264, B. Gálvez to J. Gálvez, Havana, 7 June 1783.

16. It should be noted that problems with the New Providence campaign and complaints by the Spanish navy were not the only charges facing Cagigal. He was seriously tainted by his stubborn defense of Miranda and by the contraband scandal that involved his aide-de-camp. See his lengthy *residencia*, a judicial review that all major Spanish officials had to undergo at the end of an assignment, AHN, CS 20901–20919, 21187, 21220–21222.

17. Miranda, *Democracy in America*, 19–22. Brailsford was no stranger to duels; see Henry Laurens to James Laurens, Westminister, 13 May 1772, *The Papers of Henry Laurens*, 8:306–07. Harsh memories of the New Providence campaign also existed on the Spanish side; see AHN, Estado 3887, exp. 1, letter 136, Vicente Manuel de Zéspedes to Antonio Valdés, St. Augustine, 1 Oct. 1788.

CHAPTER 4

1. It is not clear precisely when Claraco became governor of New Providence. Cagigal's instructions for Claraco were dated 22 May, but Claraco's signature on decrees can be dated from 15 May. The captain general was so busy organizing the return convoy that Claraco may well have assumed his post before Cagigal's departure on May 24. Nevertheless, until Cagigal left Nassau he was the principal Spanish official of the Bahamas. Raymundo Andrés was always referred to as interim governor. AGI, IG 1583, num. 76, Cagigal to B. Gálvez, Havana, 11 June 1782. AGI, Estado 6–3, Declaration of Raimundo Andrés, Havana, 14 July 1785. PRO, CO23/25/253–54, Proclamation of Antonio Claraco, New Providence, 15 May 1782. AGI, Cuba 1304, fs. 383–384, Ynstrucción para el governador de Providencia, Cagigal, New Providence, 22 May 1782.

2. AGI, Cuba 1368–A, Relación de la artillería [et al.] que han entrega a D. Tomás Sabala para su transporte a la Havana, New Providence, Claraco, 13 July 1782. AGI, Cuba 1368–A, Relación de la artillería [et al.] que se le han entregada a Dn. Manuel Macía para su transporte a la Havana, New Providence, Claraco, 13 July 1782.

3. A May 1782 census of the Bahama Islands showed a total population throughout the colony of 3,950 individuals, 2,750 of which resided on New Providence. The census further listed 505 men capable of bearing arms, of whom 270 lived on New Providence. PRO, PRO 30/55/41, Return of Inhabitants on the Bahama Islands, John Wilson [New Providence, May 1782]. For a slightly different count, see AGI, SD 2085–B, num. 133–H, Estado con que ha capitulado la Ysla de Providencia [Nassau, n.d.]. AGI, Cuba 165–A, Estado que manifiesta la tropa de guarnición, Claraco, New Providence, 23 Jan. 1783. AGI, Cuba 165–A, Estado que manifiesta las fuerzas maritimas, Claraco, New Providence, 23 Jan. 1783.

4. Claraco was born in Jaca (Aragon) and at this time held a captain's rank in the Regiment of Guadalajara. Andrés served in Miranda's regiment (Aragon). AGMS, Leg. C–2844, num. 1.1, Hoja de servicios de Antonio Claraco, Manuel Molina, [Dec. 1819].

5. The total number of exchequer positions in New Providence is not known. There could have been as many as 12, possibly more if servants are counted. However, the three principal posts for the treasury were the treasurer (*tesorero*), assistant treasurer (*subdelegado*), and comptroller (*contador*). The personnel in these positions rotated during the Spanish occupation. In practice, the treasurer and comptroller were the key officials because the *subdelegado* post was held by the governor. All three had keys to the treasure deposit box, and all three had to approve expenditures. AGI, Cuba 165–A, f. 29, Estado [de la] caja fuerte, Claraco, New Providence, 18 Apr. 1783.

6. AGI, Cuba 1304, fs. 400–402v, [Cagigal] to Claraco, Havana, 20 June, 1782. AGI, Cuba 1304, fs. 416–416v, Dictamen of Juan Cristosomo de Acosta, New Providence, 21 June 1782. AGI, Cuba 1304, fs. 427–428v, Claraco to Cagigal, New Providence, 25 June 1782. AGI, Cuba 1304, fs. 466–466v, Claraco to Cagigal, New Providence, 27 Aug. 1782.

7. Andrés received his appointment on 24 August and arrived in Nassau on 19 September. AGI, Cuba 1304, fs. 475–475v, [Cagigal] to Claraco, Havana, 24 Aug. 1782. AGI, Cuba 1304, f. 473, Claraco to Cagigal, New Providence, 25 Sept. 1782.

8. There was a second priest in New Providence, a Dominican by the name of José de Cardenas. Conveniently, O'Reilly happened to be in Havana on his way to West Florida when he was sidetracked to Nassau for the duration of the war. O'Reilly later played a key role in the reintroduction of Catholicism to East Florida. The Anglican priest James Barker stayed on the island at least until January 1783. He performed several baptisms but, strangely, no marriages. AGI, Cuba 1304, fs. 524–25, Andrés to Cagigal, New Providence, 10 Nov. 1782. AGI, SD 2084, num. 1011, Urriza to J. Gálvez, Havana, 23 Oct. 1782. AGI, Cuba 1304, fs. 390–390v, Claraco to Cagigal, New Providence, 3 June 1782. AGI, Cuba 1304, fs. 445–56, Claraco to Cagigal, New Providence, 1 July 1782. Michael V. Gannon, *The Cross in the Sand: The Early Catholic Church in Florida, 1513–1870*, 89–91, 95–97. BPRO, Christ Church, Baptisms and Marriages, Book 1 (1733–1843).

9. Downham and William Newton may have been among these; see chap. 2, n. 9.

10. The *Entradas y Salidas* (arrivals and departures) for Havana illustrate how often the Newtons sailed in and out of Nassau. William Woodsides, another of the pilots who led Gillon's convoy to Nassau, became harbor captain (*capitán del puerto*). George Townson, a ship captain who ran messages from Havana to Nassau for Cagigal, obtained special trading privileges with Cuba. AGI, IG 2421, Cuba 1332, SD 1234–1237, Entradas y Salidas [Havana, May 1782 to May 1783]. PRO, CO23/10/273–273v, Certificate of John Pratt, Bahama Islands, 13 Mar. 1780.

11. PRO, CO23/26/25, A Return of the Civil Officer, William Bradford, Bahama Islands, 8 May 1782.

12. Although the actual letters seem to have disappeared, the Spaniards kept an inventory of their correspondence with local officials on Harbour and Eleuthera Islands. On at least one occasion the so-called governor of Harbour Island paid a visit to the Spaniards in Nassau. AGI, Cuba 1368–A, Inventario de los asuntos militares y civiles, Claraco, New Providence, 18 Jan. 1783. AGI, Cuba 1304, fs. 411–411v, Claraco to Cagigal, New Providence, 14 June 1782.

13. Lydia Austin Parrish, "Records of Some Southern Loyalists: Being a Collection of Manuscripts about Some Eighty Families, Most of Whom Immigrated to the Bahamas during and after the American Revolution," 163, 423. PRO, CO23/25/182–85v, Minutes of the Court, Nassau, 12 [?] 1784. PRO, CO23/25/245–56, Bradford to Lord Sydney, New Providence, 30 Sept. 1784.

14. The treasury records for New Providence show how many Bahamians did business with the Spaniards. Miller was selling flour to the new conquerors within weeks of the capitulation. AGI, Estado 6–3, Liquidación de cargo y data, Manuel

de Cartas, Havana, 18 July 1786. AGI, Cuba 702, fs. 78–83v, Relación, Juan Rouset, Havana, 24 May 1783.

15. AGI, Cuba 1304, fs. 385–87, Claraco to Cagigal, New Providence, 25 May 1782.

16. Shipping between Havana and Nassau from May 1782 to April 1783:

	Ships Entering Havana from Nassau	Ships Leaving Havana for Nassau
May	1	2
June	21	4
July	22	6
Aug.	5	0
Sept.	6	8
Oct.	1	0
Nov.	13	1
Dec.	1	0
Jan.	0	4
Feb.	2	0
Mar.	2	2
Apr.	1	2

Sources: AGI, IG 2421, Cuba 1332, SD 1234–1237, *Entradas y Salidas* [Havana, May 1782 to May 1783]. In addition to the Havana trade some 18 ships left Nassau as truce flags for English controlled port. See AGI, Cuba 1368–A, Noticia de los flagatruzes que han salida de este puerto. . . , Claraco, New Providence, 18 Jan. 1783.

17. The first four months of 1782 saw as many prizes taken into Nassau as had been condemned there for all of 1781.

Prizes Condemned in the Bahamian Vice Admiralty Courts

Year	Ships
1778	12
1779	61
1780	35
1781	31
1782 (Jan.–May 8)	33
Total	172

Source: PRO, CO23/26/17–21v, A True Copy of Vessels and Cargoes Condemned . . . [by] the Vice Admiralty Court . . . , Pratt, [New Providence, n.d.].

18. Two Dutch ships complete the total for ships condemned in Nassau. Although the available documentation (see n. 17 above) does not clarify this point, Bahamian corsairs were not responsible for all the ships brought before the admiralty court in Nassau. For number of corsairs, see Memorial from John Boyd et

al. to Gary Elliot, New Providence, 17 June 1785, in *The Papers of Panton, Leslie, and Company*, 2:418–19.

19. The three most valuable ships condemned by the vice admiralty court in Nassau were Spanish—*El Flor del Mayo* (£58,525), *El Aguila de España* (£40,000), and *Nuestra Señora de la Concepción* (£30,512). As a contrast, the next most valuable prize was a French vessel worth £24,316.

Value Of Prizes Condemned in Vice Admiralty
Court January 1778 to 8 May 1782

Country of Origin		Total Value (Pounds Sterling)	Average Value (Pounds Sterling)
Spain	15	169,352	11,290
Holland	2	18,189	9,094
France	31	249,666	8,053
U.S.	124	577,113	4,654
TOTAL	172	1,014,320	5,897

Source: see n. 17 above.

20. PRO, CO23/26/35, An Account of the Guns and Warlike Stores Taken from Alexander Roxbourgh [New Providence, n.d.].

21. PRO, CO23/26/127, Inventory of the Warlike Stores That Were Taken from John Miller [New Providence, n.d.].

22. PRO, CO23/25/253–54, Proclamation of Dn Antonio Claraco, New Providence, 15 May 1782.

23. *Archivo Miranda*, 5:133–35. AGI, Cuba 1304, fs. 423–423v, Claraco to Cagigal, New Providence, 25 June 1782.

24. Thomas Roker reported that his corsair was carrying $5,200 in prize money when the Spaniards captured Nassau. The crew of his ship refused to take the privateer to a nearby British port unless Roker kept the money aboard, obviously making sure that there were funds available for their pay. PRO, CO23/26/100–03v, Narrative [of] Thomas Roker, Nassau, 22 Jan. 1785.

25. The one exception being the brig *The Fox*, which came into port as a truce ship from Bermuda. The Spaniards evidently did not confiscate that ship since Governor Claraco proposed to Havana to buy *The Fox* and to use her as a Spanish corsair. AGI, Cuba 1368–A, Claraco to Unzaga, New Providence, 23 Jan. 1783.

26. PRO, CO23/26/100–03v, Narrative [of] Thomas Roker, Nassau, 22 Jan. 1785. AGI, Cuba 1304, fs. 441–43v, Claraco to Cagigal, New Providence, 1 July 1782.

27. AGI, Estado 6–5, fs. 40v–42, Mannrique to Claraco, New Providence, 1 July 1782.

28. AGI, Cuba 1311, num. 49, Mannrique to Cagigal, New Providence, 1 July 1782. PRO, CO23/26/100–03v, Narrative [of] Thomas Roker, Nassau, 22 Jan. 1785. *Archivo Miranda*, 5:133–35. PRO, PRO 30/55/91, i10000, Memorial of Miller to Alex-

ander Leslie, Bahama Islands, 24 July 1782. AGI, Cuba 1304, fs. 441–43v, Claraco to Cagigal, New Providence, 1 July 1782.

29. AGI, Cuba 1304, fs. 439–40, Claraco to Cagigal, New Providence, 28 June 1782. AGI, Cuba 1304, fs. 423–34v, Claraco to Cagigal, New Providence, 25 June 1782. AGI, Cuba 1304, fs. 425–26v, [?] to Claraco, New Providence, 26 June 1782. *Archivo Miranda*, 5:133–35.

30. Hunter was the captain of Miller's corsair *The Unicorn*. Wheeler commanded the privateer *The Ranger*, which was active in the Bahamian waters throughout much of the war. *The Ranger's* owner was allegedly Ferguson, although he denied this. *Archivo Miranda*, 5:206–07. PRO, PRO30/55/78, i8752, Memorial of Ferguson to Guy Carleton, New York, 19 Aug. 1783.

31. These numbers come from arrest orders, letters, compensation claim lists, and vice-admiralty prize records. They should be used very cautiously, since some of the seized property involved debts owed by one corsair to another. The loser in that situation was the person who had extended the credit. A handful of Bahamians suffered both imprisonment and loss of property. Among those most affected by Spanish justice were John Miller, Thomas Roker, Alexander Roxbourgh, Robert Hunt, Joseph Hunter, Ralph Moulton, Thomas Townson, Nicholas Garner, Parr Ross, John Ferguson, and Jeremiah Tinkers. PRO, CO23/25/122–25, Observations, [n. sig., New Providence], 4 June 1784. PRO, CO23/25/255, Proclamation of Dn. Antonio Claraco y Sanz, New Providence, 1 Aug. 1782. PRO, CO23/25/256, Proclamation of Raimundo Andrés, New Providence, 30 Sept. 1782. PRO, CO23/26/17–21v, A List of Vessels and Cargoes Condemned [by] the Vice Admiralty Court, Pratt, [New Providence, 1782.]

32. The two periods of activity against privateer owners can best be seen in AGI, Estado 6–3, fs. 510v–19, Certifico de deposito [de] varios yndividuos de la nación británica, Felipe Yturrieta, [Havana, n.d.]. For a description of their confinements, see PRO, PRO30/55/91, i10000, Miller to Leslie, Bahama Island, 24 July 1782. PRO, PRO30/55/78, i8752, Ferguson to Carleton, New York, 19 Aug. 1783. PRO, CO23/26/100–03v, Narrative [of] Thomas Roker, Nassau, 22 Jan. 1785.

33. William Henry Mills, a loyalist from South Carolina, moved his family from Charleston to Nassau in 1782. Unfortunately, he had deposited nearly 21,000 reales with Alexander Roxbourgh, money which the Spanish confiscated as part of Roxbourgh's estate. Mills recovered his money only after traveling to Havana and explaining how his capital came to be held by Roxbourgh. AGI, Estado 6–3, fs. 510v–19, Certifico de deposito [de] various yndividuos de la nación británica, Yturrieta, [Havana, n.d.]. *Archivo Miranda*, 5:211, 235. PRO, AO 12/52/45–46, Memorial of William Henry Mills [n.d.].

34. John Miller, for example, smuggled a memorial to Charleston asking acquaintances there to petition British officials for help. When Cagigal recalled Governor Claraco to Havana, the captain general justified his action partly on the basis of protests from merchants in Nassau. PRO, PRO30/55/91, i10044, Memorial from Anthony Warwich and John Morris to Leslie [Charlestown, 1782?]. AGI, SD 2084, num. 294, Cagigal to J. Gálvez, Havana, 1 Oct. 1782.

35. AGI, Cuba 1336, Cagigal to Andrés, Havana, 19 Dec. 1782. AGI, Cuba

1304, fs. 540–41, Instrucción a Dn. Raymondo Andrés [Cagigal], Havana, 2 Sept. 1782.

36. AGI, Cuba 1304, fs. 476–77, Andrés to Cagigal, New Providence, 25 Sept. 1782.

37. AGI, Cuba 1304, fs. 476–77, Andrés to Cagigal, New Providence, 25 Sept. 1782. PRO, CO23/26/111–19, The Case of John Miller [New Providence?, n.d.].

38. PRO, CO23/26/111–19, The Case of John Miller [New Providence, n.d.]. PRO, CO23/26/145–49v, George Stoney to Captain General, Frigate *The Fox*, 9 Aug. 1783.

39. PRO, CO23/26/100–03v, Narrative [of] Thomas Roker, Nassau, 22 Jan. 1785. PRO, CO23/26/124–26v, The Royal Treasury of His Catholic Majesty, Debt to John Miller [Havana, n.d.].

40. For an idea of how much the French drained the Havana exchequer, see Lewis, "Las Damas de la Havana," 83–99, and AGI, Cuba 1368–A, Urriza to [Unzaga], Havana, 25 Mar. 1783.

41. AGI, Cuba 165–A, f. 7, Claraco to Unzaga, New Providence, 23 Jan. 1783.

42. Detailed Spanish financial records for New Providence exist only for the period from 21 September 1782 to the departure of the last exchequer officials in late 1783. Since the period from 8 May 1782 to 20 September 1782 was a busy one for Spaniards in Nassau, the percentages shown in the chart below should be viewed with caution. Supplementary documentation does show, however, that the financial records after 21 September include most, if not all, property confiscated from those accused of privateering. Nevertheless, the percentage given for income from those accused of illegal privateering is probably too large.

Sources of Spanish Treasury Income in New Providence

21 Sept. 1782–7 Nov. 1783

(Amounts listed in pesos. Percentages
rounded off, totaling slightly more than 100 percent)

Residents Accused Of Illegal Privateering	Contraband Seized	Loans to Exchequer	Import Taxes	Sale of Treasury Goods
220,035*	16,259	73,204	23,564	19,958
(62%)	(5%)	(21%)	(7%)	(6%)

*This amount does not include the value of personal property seized. It does, however, include several types of capital: 1) 151,259 pesos in the form of bills of exchange, 2) 34,610 pesos in various currencies held by those imprisoned, and 3) 34,166 pesos from debts owed those jailed.

Sources: AGI, Estado 6–3, Certifico de deposito [de] varios yndividuos de la nación británica, Yturrieta [Havana, n.d.]. AGI, Estado 6–3, Liquidación de cargo y data [de Nueva Providencia], Manuel de Cartas, Havana, 18 July 1786.

43. AGI, Cuba 1336, f. 366, Claraco to Unzaga, New Providence, 23 Jan. 1783. AGI, Cuba 1336, f. 368, [Unzaga] to Claraco, Havana, 24 Mar. 1783.

CHAPTER 5

1. Spanish Garrison Muster for 22 May 1782:

Regiment	Troops	Officers	Total
España	161	37	198[a]
Corona	96	8	104[b]
Artillery	9	2	11
Total	266	47	313[c]

[a]Listed as 189 in original muster.
[b]Listed as 96 in original muster.
[c]Listed as 296 in original muster.

Source: AGI, Cuba 1336, f. 450, Estado [de] guarnición, Juan Nepumeceno de Quesada, New Providence, 22 May 1782.

2. AGI, Cuba 165–A, fs. 214–22, Declaration of José de la Hoz, La Palma, Mallorca, 9 Sept. 1788.

3. The seven Spanish ships were the *Reyna de los Angeles* (packet), *La Resolución* (brig), *San Diego* (launch), *Correo de Cádiz* (packet), *San Antonio de Padua* (launch), *San Bernardo* (launch), and *San Juan Evangelista* (launch). Not counting sailors assigned to shore duty for such tasks as gathering supplies and repairing sails, their combined crews amounted to 134 men. AGI, Cuba 1336, fs. 451, Estado [de] todas clases que existían en la casa fuerte, [Claraco, New Providence], 18 Apr. 1783.

4. AGI, Cuba 1304, fs. 528–29v, Andrés to Cagigal, New Providence, 20 Dec. 1782.

5. AGI, Cuba 1304, fs. 390–93v, Claraco to Cagigal, New Providence, 3 June 1782.

6. AGI, Cuba 1304, fs. 423–423v, Claraco to Cagigal, New Providence, 25 June 1782. AGI, Cuba 1304, fs.441–43v, Claraco to Cagigal, New Providence, 1 July 1782.

7. AGI, Cuba 1304, fs. 407–09v, Claraco to Cagigal, New Providence, 14 June 1782.

8. AGI, Cuba 1304, fs. 528–29v, Andrés to Cagigal, New Providence, 20 Dec. 1782. AGI, Cuba 165–A, fs. 126–32, Declaration of Gaspar de Burgos, Mexico, 20 July 1787. AGI, Cuba 165–A, fs. 214–22, Declaration of de la Hoz, La Palma, Mallorca, 9 Sept. 1788.

9. AGI, Cuba 1304, fs. 528–29v, Andrés to Cagigal, New Providence, 20 Dec. 1782. AGI, Cuba 165–A, fs. 7v–8v, Claraco to Unzaga, New Providence, 21 Feb. 1783. AGI, Cuba 165–A, fs. 9v–11, Claraco to Unzaga, New Providence, 27 Mar. 1783. AGI, Cuba 165–A, fs. 11–12, Claraco to Unzaga, 28 Mar. 1783.

10. AGI, Cuba 1368–A, Noticia de los flagatruzes que han salida de este puerto, Claraco, New Providence, 18 Jan. 1783.

11. AGI, Cuba 165–A, fs. 7v–8v, Claraco to Unzaga, New Providence, 21 Feb. 1783.

12. For documentation of these actions see n. 9 above.

13. J. Leitch Wright, Jr., *Florida in the American Revolution*, 118–24.

14. PRO, C05/106/147–54v, Townshend to Carleton, Whitehall, 14 Aug. 1782.

15. Except for Sandra Riley's recent work on Abaco, Rumer's role in organizing the expedition has been surprisingly overlooked by historians. This is due in great part to Andrew Deveaux's flair for publicity. Public relations pay, even in history. For Rumer's contributions see PRO, CO23/26/224, Certificate in Behalf of Robert Rumer, Sam Higgs et al., Harbour Island, 25 Apr. 1786. Also see PRO, CO23/15/163–64, Rumer to Lord Sydney, New Providence, 21 Apr. 1784; PRO, CO23/26/107, Affidavit of Robert Rumer, New Providence, 11 Mar. 1785; PRO, CO23/26/207–08, Robert Sterling et al. to Anthony Stokes, Nassau, 9 Mar. 1786; PRO, CO23/26/223, Memorial of Rumer to Lord Sydney, Nassau, 21 Feb. 1786; Sandra Riley, *Homeward Bound: A History of the Bahama Islands to 1850 with a Definitive Study of Abaco in the American Loyalist Period*, 132–35.

16. In spite of his stature as a person of note in the Bahamas and, to a lesser degree, in South Carolina, Deveaux has not received a serious biographical study. What exists for the colonel is dated and brief. See Lorenzo Sabine, *Biographical Sketches of Loyalists of the American Revolution With an Historical Essay*, 1: 377–78; Joseph Johnson, *Traditions and Reminiscences Chiefly of the American Revolution in the South: Including Biographical Sketches, Incidents and Anecdotes Few of Which Have Been Published, Particularly of Residents in the Upper Country*, 175–81; Stephen B. Barnwell, *The Story of an American Family*, 40, 52–55. Much of Deveaux's background can be reconstructed from PRO, AO12/52/17–19, Memorial of Col. Andrew Deveaux, [London, n.d.]; PRO, AO12/100/344–344v, Summary of Claim by A. Deveaux, [London], 6 July 1784; PRO, AO13/127/173–74, Memorial of A. Deveaux, [London, 8 Mar. 1784?]; PRO, AO13/127/182–182v, Memorial of A. Deveaux, London, 6 Feb. 1784.

17. Catherine S. Crary, comp., *The Price of Loyalty: Tory Writings from the Revolutionary Era*, 355. Bryan Edwards, *The History, Civil and Commercial, of the British Colonies in the West Indies*, 4: 393–94. James Grant Forbes, *Sketches, Historical and Topographical, of the Floridas; More Particularly of East Florida*, 52–53. Paul Albury, *The Story of the Bahamas*, 104–07. *Bahamas Handbook and Businessman's Annual*, 15–26.

18. Primary sources on the British side give the number of volunteers as 40–50, 65, and 70 soldiers. Most scholars, properly I think, have accepted the two larger estimates as the most accurate. Roderick Mackenzie, *Strictures on Lt. Col. Tarleton's History "Of the Campaign of 1780 and 1781, in the Southern Provinces of North America": The Recapture of the Island of New Providence*, 8–9. PRO, CO5/110/38–39v, *East Florida Gazette*, Apr. 26–May 3, 1783. Crary, *Price of Loyalty*, pp. 356–57.

19. Deveaux signed a written contract with David Fanning on 3 March 1783 to recruit soldiers. This contract has survived. Fanning, an experienced and somewhat notorious loyalist from North Carolina, collected nearly thirty volunteers for Deveaux. His entire group, unfortunately, missed the rendezvous with Deveaux

and never participated in the campaign. See Fanning, *The Narrative of Col. David Fanning*, ed. Lindley S. Butler, 83–84.

20. Besides the Fanning contract, a second written agreement has survived, one made with the corsair captains signed on 22 April 1783, four days after the fall of Nassau. Since parts of this corsair agreement clearly conflict with the Fanning contract, it is likely that most of Deveaux's followers had no formal arrangement governing their service or reward. See PRO, CO23/26/104–104v, Deposition of Daniel Wheeler, Thomas Atwood, Bahama Island, 24 Feb. 1785.

21. The corsair brig *Apollo* (Captain Jonas Ridley) and the schooner *Rodney* (Captain Archibald Fisher) joined the blockade of Nassau on 17 April. PRO, CO23/26/40–41, Sworn Statement of Thomas Dow, William Bradford, New Providence, 21 May 1783. Thomas Brown, perhaps the most famous of Georgia's loyalists, was part owner of the *Whitby Warrior*, named after his hometown. Edward J. Cashin, *The King's Ranger: Thomas Brown and the American Revolution on the Southern Frontier*, 162.

22. Mackenzie, *Strictures*, 9–10.

23. Deveaux, Rumer, and Samuel Higgs (Captain of the Harbour Island militia) recruited on Harbour Island. Alexander Mackenzie did the same for Eleuthera Island. Mackenzie, *Strictures*, 10–11. PRO, CO23/26/224, Certificate in behalf of Robert Rumer, Sam Higgs et al., Harbour Island, 25 Apr. 1786. PRO, CO5/110/38–39v, *East Florida Gazette*, 26 Apr.–3 May 1783. Rumer's friendship with Higgs can be also seen in the latter's will. BPRO, Supreme Court, Wills, Will of Samuel Higgs, Harbour Island, 3 Sept. 1792.

24. PRO, PR030/55/41, num. 4705, Return of Inhabitants on the Bahama Islands, John Wilson, [New Providence, May 1782]. The estimate of 120 men from Harbour Island (some 30 over the number listed who could supposedly bear arms) and 50 from Eleuthera comes from PRO, CO5/110/38–39v, *East Florida Gazette*, 26 April–3 May 1783, and Mackenzie, *Strictures*, 10–11.

25. Nearly all the Spanish witnesses called to testify in Claraco's court-martial after the war noted the presence of large numbers of blacks and mulattoes in Deveaux's force. Most English sources, curiously enough, did not. Evidently many white soldiers left Claraco's army immediately after Claraco's surrender. See AGI, Cuba 165–A, fs. 190v–203, Declaration of Tomás de Novoa y Feyjóo, Puerto Rico, 26 Nov. 1787. White officers stayed under arms for at least several months. PRO, AO13/59/3, Affidavit of Donald Ferguson, Abaco, 17 Apr. 1786.

26. AGI, Cuba 165–A, fs. 190v–203, Declaration of Novoa, Puerto Rico, 26 Nov. 1787. PRO, CO23/26/61–70, Claraco to Maxwell, New Providence, 13 July 1784.

27. PRO, CO23/26/40–41, Declaration of Thomas Dow, New Providence, 21 May 1783. PRO, CO23/26/42–43, Declaration of Daniel Wheeler, New Providence, 21 May 1783.

28. After the war Claraco accused Deveaux of knowing about the peace before the English colonel left St. Augustine, an accusation that was most likely not true. He also maintained that the English leader arrested two merchant captains at Harbour Island before the attack on Nassau because these two gentlemen had just

come from Antigua with newspapers containing news of the preliminary agreement signed in Europe. This last charge probably had some substance to it. Claraco had months of idle time after the siege to dig up such information in Nassau. PRO, CO23/26/61–70, Claraco to Maxwell, New Providence, 13 July 1784.

29. AGI, Cuba 165–A, fs. 9v–11, Claraco to Unzaga, New Providence, 27 Mar. 1783.

30. AGI, Cuba 165–A, fs. 255v–61v, Declaration of Claraco, Havana, 7 Jan. 1789.

31. AGI, SD 1236, Entradas y salidas de Abril, Havana, 30 Apr. 1783. AGI, Cuba 1336, fs. 470–470v, [Unzaga] to Governor of the Bahamas, Havana, 2 Apr. 1783.

32. AGI, Cuba 165–A, fs. 19–22v, Consejo de Guerra, Manuel de Sotarriba et al., New Providence, 18 Apr. 1783. AGI, Cuba 165–A, fs. 255v–61v, Declaration of Claraco, Havana, 7 Jan. 1789.

33. Although some historians have claimed that the residents of East Florida were notified as early as February 1783 to plan on moving from that province once the war ended, official news of the peace did not reach St. Augustine until 21 April 1783 (or slightly before), the date on which the *East Florida Gazette* ran a special edition announcing the end of hostilities. See Charlton W. Tebeau, *A History of Florida*, 87; Wilbur Henry Siebert, *Loyalists in East Florida, 1774–1785; The Most Important Documents Pertaining Thereto, Edited with an Accompanying Narrative*, 1: 134.

34. AGI, Cuba 165–A, fs. 19–22v, Consejo de Guerra, Manuel de Sotarriba et al., New Providence, 18 Apr. 1783. AGI, Cuba 165–A, fs. 76v–81, Declaration of Juan Yzquierdo, Havana, 31 May 1785. AGI, Cuba 165–A, fs. 120v–24v, Declaration of Martín Armossa, St. Augustine, 9 Dec. 1786. AGI, Cuba 165–A, fs. 383v–84v, Declaration of Pedro Sarlate, Havana, 16 Sept. 1783.

35. AGI, Cuba, 165–A, fs. 19–22v, Consejo de Guerra, Manuel de Sotarriba et al., New Providence, 18 Apr. 1783.

36. See the letters and declarations of Antonio Claraco y Sanz, Bernardo Guerrero, Antonio Pasqual Vidal, Juan Yzquierdo, Juan Monroy, José de Soto, Martín Armossa, Manuel Gutiérrez, José Lara, Angel Pavia in AGI, Cuba 165–A, fs. 13v–14v, 19–22v, 53v–56v, 72–76v, 76v–81, 84–87v, 96v–109, 120v–24v, 172v–79, 179–84, 184–90, 255v–61v, 385–91v.

37. AGI, Cuba 165–A, fs. 381–83v, Declaration of Armossa, Havana, 2 Sept. 1783.

38. For sources, see n. 36 above.

39. AGI, Cuba 165–A, fs. 53v–56v, Declaration of Guerrero, Havana, 9 May 1785.

40. Several defenders of Fort Montague testified after the war that there were native-speaking Spaniards who participated on the British side. Claraco learned the identity of several of these individuals after the contest and sent secret orders to Havana to have one of these men, who unwisely accompanied a truce ship to Cuba, arrested and imprisoned. Minorca was a British possession throughout most

of the eighteenth century. AGI, Cuba 165–A, fs. 48–53v, 53v–56v, 72–76v, 213–22, Declarations of Juan Safores, Bernardo Guerrero, Antonio Pasqual Vidal, and José de la Hoz.

41. Testimony of the three ship captains posted at Fort Montague is found in AGI, Cuba 165–A, fs. 72–76v, 120v–24, 361–66v, Declarations of Antonio Pasqual Vidal, Martín de Armossa, and Juan de Menchaca.

42. The missing match played a crucial role in the defense of Fort Montague. Its absence prevented the fort from firing on the enemy, thereby warning Nassau at the same time. It also reinforced British belief that the fort had been caught napping and thereby could be taken easily. Lastly, the hunt for the match delayed the lighting of the mines and increased the likelihood that the fuses could be caught in time. Numerous eyewitnesses noted the match's absence, but only one gave a reasonable explanation of what had happened to it (that it had been sent to the recently arrived felucca). Once again the timing of events worked to the detriment of the Spanish forces. AGI, Cuba 165–A, fs. 84–87v, Declaration of Juan Monroy, Havana, 3 June 1785.

43. AGI, Cuba 165–A, fs. 96v–109, Declaration of José de Soto, Havana, 7 Aug. 1786.

44. The suspected traitor was Sergeant Vicente Roche, one of the captured soldiers at Fort Montague, who did not return to his regiment after the Spanish prisoners were released by Deveaux. Knowing what he might be charged with, Roche quite possibly decided not to risk his freedom by returning to the colors. AGI, Cuba 165–A, fs. 19–22v, Consejo de Guerra, New Providence, 18 Apr. 1783. AGI, Cuba 165–A, fs. 84–87v, Declaration of Monroy, Havana, 3 June 1785. AGI, Cuba 165–A, fs. 150v–56, Declaration of Miguel del Campo, Mexico, 9 Aug. 1787. AGI, Cuba 165–A, fs. 179–84, Declaration of José Lara, Mexico, 31 Aug. 1787. The most detailed and best British account of the attack on Fort Montague remains Mackenzie, *Strictures*, 12–14. Although dated and little used, George Nester Trichoche's article on the campaign is very insightful; see Trichoche, "La Prise de Nassau (Bahamas) par les Loyalistes de la Caroline de Sud en 1783."

45. Illness was a serious problem with any Caribbean garrison, particularly if it was composed of new troops from Europe. The Bahama garrison, however, was reasonably well-seasoned and not likely to succumb to such deadly epidemics as yellow fever. Nevertheless, lesser diseases took their toll throughout the occupation. At one point Governor Andrés reported that half of his effectives were either sick or recovering from illness. The Spanish hospital records show a curious drop of patients on 13 April, a fall from 54 persons on 12 April to 15 patients for 13 April. If the documents did not indicate otherwise, such a sharp change would seem to indicate that the Spaniards anticipated an attack on 13 April, leaving in the hospital only those who were too ill to contribute to the defense of New Providence. AGI, Cuba 1304, f. 522, Andrés to Cagigal, New Providence, 25 Oct. 1782. AGI, Cuba 165–A, fs. 45v–46, Extracto de los enfermos que existieron en el hospital real, Manuel Vizcaya, Havana, 8 July 1785.

46. From the original garrison of 296 soldiers (corrected to 313, see n. 1 above), Claraco reported 36 deaths during the occupation—leaving 260 (277) in April 1783. From this total should be subtracted the two captives taken at Fort Montague

and those who remained in the hospital during the siege (13 to 14 patients), giving a final figure for those in the *Casa Fuerte* of 244 or 245 (261 or 262). Spanish records show that 155 sailors and shore help (corrected to 157) were assigned to Nassau. The Spanish navy lost 34 of these as prisoners at Fort Montague, and 13 had been sent earlier to Cuba—leaving 108 (110) in Nassau. Thus a total force of some 368 to 387 Spaniards existed in Nassau to resist Deveaux after the first day of the siege. By the end of the campaign Claraco listed 90 soldiers and 30 sailors as too ill to fight. If that were true, the governor's total number of effectives would have been somewhere between 248 and 267 men. On 18 April, the last full day of fighting, Claraco reported 235 healthy men to garrison his works. See AGI, Cuba 1336, f. 451, Estado [de] todas clases que existían en la casa fuerte, [Claraco, New Providence], 18 Apr. 1783. AGI, Cuba 165–A, fs. 22v–23v, Claraco to Unzaga, New Providence, 19 May 1783.

47. Since the Deveaux expedition was an informal collection of men, the colonel kept no records of the total number of individuals involved. For the period up to the capture of Fort Montague, however, the English probably numbered around 300 men, including sailors who could be detached for land duty. After that point Deveaux's followers may well have swelled to 400 or 500 in all. See Mackenzie, *Strictures*, 11, and Crary, *Price of Loyalty*, 356–57.

48. For an entertaining taste of this type of history, see such older works as Forbes, *Sketches*, 52–54; Siebert, *Loyalists in East Florida*, 1: 146–47; Johnson, *Traditions*, 179–81; Johann David Schoepf, *Travels in the Confederation*, 2: 263, 316; Edwards, *History of the British Colonies*, 4: 393–94; George R. Fairbanks, *History of Florida*, 237–38. Most modern historians are far more cautious about the more flamboyant claims concerning Deveaux. For some exceptions see Crary, *Price of Loyalty*, 354–55; Albury, *Story of the Bahamas*, 104–07, and *Bahama Handbook*, 15–26. Also contrast the description of this event in two new works, both excellent, on Southern loyalists: Cashin, *King's Ranger*, 162, and Robert Stansbury Lambert, *South Carolina Loyalists in the American Revolution*, 262.

49. In all the Spanish testimony gathered after the war about the campaign, much of it very hostile to Antonio Claraco, only a few witnesses made any mention of Deveaux's supposed Indian auxiliaries or any of the other deceptions practiced by the British leader. This may well mean, of course, that these tricks worked so well that the Spaniards never realized that they had been deceived. Considering how long some of the Spaniards remained in Nassau after the conquest, however, it would have been unlikely that such actions would have been kept from them. For soldiers who had fought at Pensacola, Indians held little novelty or mystery. Spaniards who testified about the siege were far more struck by the number of blacks, mulattoes, and local residents in Deveaux's army than anything else. AGI, Cuba 165–A, fs. 120v–25v, Declaration of Armossa, St. Augustine, 9 Dec. 1786.

50. British sources on this point limit themselves to the briefest of explanations. See Crary, *Price of Loyalty*, 356–57; Mackenzie, *Strictures*, 15; PRO CO23/15/163–64, Rumer to Lord Sydney, New Providence, 21 Apr. 1784; PRO, CO5/110/38–39v, *East Florida Gazette*, 26 Apr.–3 May 1783.

51. AGI, Cuba 165–A, fs. 18–18v, Treguas establecidas entre [Claraco y Deveaux], [Claraco and Deveaux, New Providence, 14 Apr. 1783].

52. Mackenzie, *Strictures*, 18; AGI, Cuba 165–A, fs. 17–18, Claraco to Unzaga, New Providence, 5 May 1783. AGI, Cuba 165–A, fs. 48–53v, Declaration of Safores, Havana, 8 May 1785.

53. AGI, Cuba 165–A, fs. 96v–109, Declaration of Soto, Havana, 7 Aug. 1786. AGI, Cuba 165–A, fs. 190v–203, Declaration of Novoa, Puerto Rico, 26 Nov. 1787. AGI, Cuba 165–A, fs. 214–22, Declaration of de la Hoz, La Palma, Mallorca, 9 Sept. 1788.

54. There were not many Americans in the *Casa Fuerte*, estimates ranging from a low of 4 or 5 to a high of 20 to 25. Nevertheless, they apparently argued for an attack on Fort Montague, offering to participate. At least two American ships attempted to leave Nassau during the siege, one taking Claraco's appeal for help to Havana. PRO, CO23/26/40–41, Declaration of Dow, New Providence, 21 May 1783. AGI, Cuba 165–A, fs. 245v–52, Declaration of Juan de Menchaca, Cádiz, 2 Oct. 1788. AGI, Cuba 165–A, fs. 56–60v, Declaration of Francisco Samundy, Havana, 19 May 1785. AGI, Cuba 165–A, fs. 96v–109, Declaration of Soto, Havana, 7 Aug. 1786. AGI, Cuba 165–A, fs. 190v–203, Declaration of Novoa, Puerto, Rico, 26 Nov. 1787.

55. AGI, Cuba 165–A, fs. 266–70, Declaration of Claraco, Havana, 9 Jan. 1789.

56. Mackenzie, *Strictures*, 18.

57. For different versions of this ambush, see Mackenzie, *Strictures*, 16; and AGI, Cuba 165–A, fs. 48–53v, Declaration of Safores, Havana, 8 May 1785; AGI, Cuba 165–A, fs. 17–18, Claraco to Unzaga, New Providence, 5 May 1783.

58. AGI, Cuba 165–A, fs. 91–95v, Declaration of Antonio Azoñes, Havana, 21 June 1785.

59. AGI, Cuba 165–A, fs. 17–18, Claraco to Unzaga, New Providence, 5 May 1783. AGI, Cuba 165–A, fs. 96v–109, Declaration of Soto, Havana, 7 Aug. 1786. AGI, Cuba 165–A, fs. 150v–56, Declaration of Campo, Mexico, 9 Aug. 1787. AGI, Cuba 165–A, fs. 385–91v, Declaration of Soto, Havana, 24 Nov. 1783.

60. AGI, Cuba 165–A, fs 391v–97, Declaration of Arias, Havana, 24 Nov. 1783.

61. AGI, Cuba 165–A, fs. 340–45v, Consejo de Guerra, Manuel de Sotarriba et al, Casa Fuerte, 18 Apr. 1783.

62. Almon, *Remembrancer*, 2: 144.

CHAPTER 6

1. One of the rare failures in the career of Horatio Nelson, later famous as Lord Nelson, was his effort to recapture the Turks Islands from the French in March 1783. See Carola Oman, *Nelson*, 50–51.

2. In the case of East Florida, Vicente Manuel de Zéspedes, the new Spanish governor, arrived in St. Augustine on 27 June 1784. The last British governor of East Florida, however, did not depart until November 1785. According to the preliminary and final Treaty of Paris, the Spaniards were to turn over the Bahamas within three months of the final ratification (12 September 1783). For an accessible copy of the treaties between Spain and England, see Francis Gardiner Davenport

and Charles Oscar Paullin, *European Treaties Bearing on the History of the United States and Its Dependencies*, 4: 150–51, 158–61.

3. In theory the council should have had 12 members, but the Bahamian version in 1782 had only 8 (John Brown, William Bradford, Robert Sterling, Robert Hunt, Andrew Symmer, Thomas Atwood, Parr Ross, and George McKenzie). Because the council had been such a center of opposition to earlier governors during the war, the colonial ministry in London had left the council short so that the new head of the colony, Governor John Maxwell, could recommend future members whose loyalty would be beyond question. In addition to the current council members there were other Bahamians, such as John Miller, who had served on the council previously and still resided in the colony. PRO, CO23/25/21–21v, Maxwell to Germain, New Providence, 15 Mar. 1781. PRO, CO23/25/23–25, Germain to Maxwell, New Providence, 4 July 1781.

4. PRO, CO5/111/180–81v, Hunt to Carleton, New Providence, 27 Oct. 1783. Parrish, "Records," 225. Parrish gives the date of 11 April for the beginning of the Board of Police. This is two days before Deveaux's assault on Fort Montague. Considering Deveaux's propensity to improvise on the spot and considering the overwhelming task of organizing an attack, the Parrish date is suspect. Furthermore, many of the men on the original board were still in Nassau and would have been unable to consult with the militia colonel about a new government.

5. British Museum, Additional Manuscripts 42414, pp. 40–42, Carleton to McArthur, New York, 29 July 1783. McArthur's junior officer was Lt. John Wilson, who also had orders from Carleton to report on the Bahamas. PRO, PRO30/55/81, i9105, McArthur to Carleton, St. Augustine, 12 September 1783. Riley, *Homeward Bound*, 136, 158–59.

6. PRO, CO26/10/1–3, Address of Maxwell to Assembly, [Nassau], 20 Apr. 1784. PRO, CO26/10/3–4, Reply to Maxwell, [Nassau], 21 Apr. 1784.

7. The Newton family is a principal example. Downham Newton and William (Jeremiah?) Newton were two of the pilots who led Gillon and the Spaniards to Nassau. During the occupation a Downham Newton and Jeremiah Newton were frequently listed in port records as captains of boats traveling to and from Havana. After the war Newtons with these same Christian names remained active in the affairs of New Providence. It is possible, of course, that there were a number of Newtons with identical given names. AGI, IG 2421, Cuba 1332, and SD 1234–1237, Entradas y Salidas, Havana, Apr. 1782–Apr. 1783. PRO, CO23/27/41v, Journal of the General Assembly, Thomas Roker, New Providence, 11 Jan. 1787. PRO, CO23/25/182–85v, Minutes of the Court, George Bunch, Nassau, 12 [?] 1784. PRO, CO23/26/40–41, Sworn Statement of Thomas Dow, New Providence, 21 May 1783.

8. For the case against Bradford and his defense see the various documents at PRO, CO26/10/10–11 and PRO, CO23/25/245–64. Bradford was still living in the Bahamas as late as 1789. BPRO, Supreme Court, August Term, 1789, John Ferguson v. William Bradford and Susannah Helms.

9. AGI, Cuba 1336, fs. 426–27, Claraco to Unzaga, New Providence, 5 July 1783. AGI, Cuba 165–A, fs. 96v–109, Declaration of Soto, Havana, 7 Aug. 1786.

10. Exchequer records for the Spanish period in New Providence can be found at AGI, Estado 6–3, Treasury Accounts [Income and Expenses], Manuel de Cartas,

Havana, 18 July 1786. AGI, Cuba 691, Inventory of Exchequer Documents and Exchequer Income and Expenses, Yturrieta, Havana, 31 Dec. 1782.

11. Ten ships arrived in Havana from New Providence between 10 May and 15 May, 4 more came in 24 May. See AGI, SD 1236, Entradas y Salidas, Havana, 31 May 1783; AGI, Estado 6–3, Report of Claraco, Havana, 4 Oct. 1785.

12. To Claraco's credit he obviously intended to make sure his men returned to Havana before leaving himself. AGI, Cuba 1336, fs. 389–389v, Claraco to Unzaga, New Providence, 1 May 1783. AGI, Cuba 1336, fs. 399–400, Deveaux to Claraco, [New Providence, 5 May 1783].

13. AGI, Cuba 1336, fs. 430–31v, Claraco to Unzaga, New Providence, 14 July 1783. PRO, CO23/26/32–33, Hunt to Andrés, New Providence, 4 Nov. [1783].

14. PRO, CO23/26/111–19, The Case of John Miller. PRO, CO23/25/78–79, Hunt to Lord Sydney, New Providence, 15 Mar. 1784. Parrish, "Records," 226.

15. AGI, Cuba 1336, fs. 428–428v, Claraco to Unzaga, New Providence, 27 Aug. 1783.

16. For the departure of various Spaniards from Nassau see AGI, Cuba 1336, f. 353, Andrés to Hunt, aboard American Schooner *Maryland*, 31 Oct. 1783; AGI, Cuba 1336, fs. 353–54v, Hunt to Andrés, [New Providence, n.d.]; AGI, Cuba 1336, f. 381, Claraco to Unzaga, New Providence, 22 Mar. 1784; AGI, Cuba 1336, fs. 386–87, Claraco to Unzaga, New Providence, 28 Apr. 1784; AGI, Cuba 1336, fs. 432–432v, Claraco to Unzaga, New Providence, 8 Sept. 1783; PRO, CO23/26/83–84, Maxwell to Unzaga, New Providence, 29 Apr. 1784.

17. Maxwell was keenly sensitive to the fate of his predecessor, Governor Browne, who had been driven from office by local opposition in 1780. As a result he backed away from conflict, even when he was right on an issue. For an example of Maxwell's unwillingness to provoke those who needed some restraint, see his letter about Deveaux's supporters at PRO, CO23/25/175, Maxwell to Sydney, New Providence, 30 Aug. 1784.

18. PRO, CO23/25/119–21v, Claraco to Maxwell, New Providence, 28 Apr. 1784.

19. PRO, CO23/25/120, Claraco to Maxwell, New Providence, 29 Apr. 1784.

20. PRO, CO23/26/61–70, Claraco to Maxwell, New Providence, 13 July 1784.

21. PRO, FO 185/2/11, Sydney to Maxwell, Whitehall, 6 Aug. 1784.

22. Alexander Roxbourgh, one of the Bahamian merchants then in Havana to press claims against the Spanish exchequer, heard rumors that Claraco would attempt to break his parole. He warned Maxwell in a letter to be extremely vigilant about his Spanish hostage. Considering that Roxbourgh was dealing with the intendant's office in Havana, it is not inconceivable that treasury officials were the source of Roxbourgh's rumors. PRO, CO23/26/71–72, Roxbourgh to Maxwell, Havana, 2 Aug. 1784. In one of those ironies of history Andrew Deveaux, Claraco's initial captor, escaped imprisonment in South Carolina during the war in much the same manner that the Spaniard did, pledging not to break house arrest and then doing so. Deveaux found such action easy to do; Claraco obviously did not. Barnwell, *An American Family,* 54. PRO, AO13/127/179, Affidavit of John Johnson, Lincoln Inn Fields, 24 June 1786.

23. *The London Gazette*, 26 July–29 July 1783, pp. 1–3.

24. Discussions had taken place as early as September, but Campo's first formal protest was evidently in October. AGS, Estado 8151, Campo to Floridablanca, London, 17 Sept. 1783. AGS, Estado 8151, [Campo] to Fox, [London], [?] Oct. 1783.

25. AGS, Estado 8151, [Campo] to Floridablanca, London, 23 May 1784.

26. AGS, Estado 8151, Floridablanca to Campo, Madrid, 3 Jan. 1784. AGS, Estado 8151, Floridablanca to Campo, San Ildefonso, 11 Aug. 1784.

27. The Spanish court indicated its satisfaction in 1784 with a proposed English apology. Evidently the British government then delayed making such regrets public. By summer of 1785 correspondence concerning this issue had stopped on both sides. AGS, Estado 8151, Floridablanca to Campo, San Ildefonso, 11 Aug. 1784. AGS, Estado 8151, [Campo] to Fraser, [London], 15 June 1785.

28. PRO, CO23/26/71–72, Roxbourgh to Maxwell, Havana, 2 Aug. 1784.

29. Miller's request was evidently made in early 1786. Yet the Spanish government knew in 1785 that some sort of diplomatic representation would probably be made on behalf of the Bahamian merchants. PRO, FO72/7/11, Memorial of Miller to Carmarthen, London, 13 Feb. 1786. AGS, Estado 8151, Sydney to Carmarthen, Whitehall, 17 June 1785.

30. PRO, FO72/2/5–6, Memorial of James Niven and Arthur Gibbons to Carmarthen, London, 7 Jan. 1784.

31. A copy of Miller's printed memorial does not seem to have survived the centuries. That it contained some undiplomatic opinions, however, is clear. PRO, FO72/8/44, Liston to Carmarthen, Aranjuez, 29 June 1786.

32. PRO, FO185/3/32, Floridablanca to Liston, Aranjuez, 4 May 1787.

33. Mier was a high-ranking member (*oficial mayor*) of the Cuban intendancy. When he traveled to New Providence is difficult to determine. Most likely the trip took place in the summer or early fall of 1783. See "Guia de Forasteros en la Habana ¡Para el Año 1781!," *Memorias de la Sociedad Económica de Amigos del País*, 15: 115. AGI, Estado 6–3, Declaration of Yturrieta, Havana, 2 Aug. 1784. AGI, Estado 6–3, Declaration of Soto, Havana, 2 Aug. 1784. AGI, Estado 6–3, Declaration of Arias, Havana, 2 Aug. 1784. AGI, Estado 6–3, Declaration of Yzquierdo, Havana, 12 Aug. 1784. AGI, Estado 6–3, Declaration of Cartas, Havana, 18 Sept. 1784.

34. AGI, Cuba 1336, fs. 342–44v, Instructions to Unzaga, 27 Aug. 1784.

35. AGI, Cuba 1336, fs. 356–57v, Andrés to Unzaga, 20 Nov. 1783.

36. AGI, Cuba 1336, f. 354, Andrés to Hunt, aboard the schooner *Sta. Ana* [sic], 5 Nov. 1783. PRO, CO23/26/32–33, Hunt to Andrés, New Providence, 4 Nov. [1783].

37. PRO, FO185/2/num. 11, Maxwell to Unzaga, New Providence, 29 Apr. 1784. AGS, Estado 8151, num. 3, J. Gálvez to Floridablanca, Palacio, 21 Mar. 1785.

38. AGI, Estado 6–3, Declaration of Claraco, Havana, 4 Oct. 1785.

39. For details of this case see AGI, Estado 6–1 to 6–5.

40. AGI, Estado 6–3, Sentencia [de Claraco], Alfonso María de Cárdenas et

al., Havana, 30 Sept. 1788. AGI, Estado 6–2, Claraco to Gardoqui, Madrid, 29 July 1794. Cartas and Yturrieta also received small fines. Cartas was ordered to pay 7 reales (less than a peso) for a mistake in accounting. Yturrieta died shortly after returning to Havana, but the treasurer's estate was accessed a penalty of 240 reales (30 pesos) for similar violations of accounting procedures.

41. AGI, Cuba 165–A, fs. 421–421v, royal order to governor of Havana, Madrid, 3 Aug. 1789.

42. AGS, GM 6091, Certification of Francisco Bordesi, Madrid, 27 Sept. 1791. AGS, GM 6091, Cristóbal de Zayas to [?], [Madrid, ? Oct. 1791].

43. AGMS, Leg. C–2844, num. 1.1, Hoja de Servicios de Antonio Claraco y Sanz, Cosme Martínez Ubago, Viaña, 11 Jan. 1820.

44. AGI, Estado 6–1, royal order to intendant of Cuba, Aranjuez, 23 June 1792. AGI, Estado 6–1, royal order to intendant of Havana, San Lorenzo, 6 Nov. 1791.

45. Evidence is contradictory whether Claraco received all of his withheld salary. Some payments were made, but the former governor was still complaining as late as 1794 that he had not received the full amount. AGI, Estado 6–4, Nota de Vidaondo, [Havana, 6 Oct. 1792]. AGI, Estado 6–2, Claraco to Gardoqui, Madrid, 29 July 1794.

46. AGMS, Leg. C–2844, num. 1.1, Hoja de Servicios de Antonio Claraco y Sanz, Cosme Martínez Ubago, Viaña, 11 Jan. 1820.

CHAPTER 7

1. Riley, *Homeward Bound*, 104–06, 131–34. Craton, *Price of Loyalty*, 158–61.

2. James A. Lewis, "Anglo-American Entrepreneurs in Havana: The Background and Significance of the Expulsion of 1784–1785," 112–26.

3. O'Fallon earned some notoriety after the war as a land speculator in the trans-Appalachian West. AHN, Estado 3887, exp. 1, letter 136, Zéspedes to Valdés, St. Augustine, 1 Oct. 1788.

4. Miranda never stopped being a soldier. However, his transition from being a soldier for Spain to one against Spain is an intriguing problem for historians. It certainly did not happen all at once. Even as late as 1785, two years after his flight from Havana, the future Precursor was corresponding with Spanish officials in an effort to explain his actions—hardly the type of activity one would expect from a resolute revolutionary. See AGS, Estado 8141, exp. 7, Miranda to Floridablanca, London, 10 Apr. 1785.

5. In a small colony like New Providence, for example, one of the tasks of the governor was to certify (to prove) wills. Claraco did this in the same fashion that his English predecessors had. See BPRO, Supreme Court, Will of Benjamin Bill, New Providence, 22 Oct. 1779.

6. Craton, *Price of Loyalty*, 176–78.

7. BPRO, Supreme Court, General Court, John Scott v. John Miller, Nassau, November Term, 1789.

8. Several partners of the famous Indian-trading firm of Panton, Leslie, and Company settled in Nassau after 1783. For a while, some of the older Bahamian firms attempted to challenge Panton's trade monopoly with the Indians in Spanish Florida. See William S. Coker and Thomas D. Watson, *Indian Traders of the Southeastern Spanish Borderlands*, 44–45, 117–20.

9. AGI, Cuba 1304, fs. 460–460v, Memorial of William Henry Mills to [Claraco], New Providence, ? Aug. 1782.

10. *Papers of Panton, Leslie, and Company*, 2: 418–30.

SOURCES CITED

PRIMARY SOURCES

Archives

Columbia, South Carolina. South Carolina State Archives (SCSA).
    Audited Accounts (AA), 118, 3031A.
    General Assembly Papers (GAP).

London. British Museum.
    Additional Manuscripts, 42414.

London. Public Record Office (PRO).
    Audit Office (AO), 12/52, 12/100, 13/59, 13/127.
    Carleton Papers (PRO 30/55), 41, 78, 81, 91.
    Colonial Office (CO), 5/106, 5/110, 5/111, 23/9, 23/10, 23/15, 23/24,
        23/25, 23/26, 23/27, 26/6, 26/10, 37/22, 137/30.
    Foreign Office (FO), 72/2, 72/7, 72/8, 185/2, 185/3.

Madrid. Archivo Histórico Nacional (AHN).
    Consejos Suprimidos (CS), 20170, 20878, 20901–20919, 21187, 21220–
        21222.
    Estado, 3884bis, 3887.

Nassau, New Providence. Public Record Office (BPRO).
    Christ Church Records, Baptisms and Marriages (1733–1843).
    Council Minutes.
    Supreme Court, General Court.
    Supreme Court, Wills.

Segovia. Archivo General Militar de Segovia (AGMS).
  Legajo (Leg.) C–2844.

Seville. Archivo General de Indias (AGI).
  Cuba, 165–A, 224–A, 691, 702, 1304, 1308, 1309, 1311, 1318, 1331,
    1332, 1336, 1340, 1368–A.
  Estado, 6–1, 6–2, 6–3, 6–4, 6–5.
  Indiferente General (IG), 1579, 1580, 1581, 1583, 1584, 2421.
  Santo Domingo (SD), 1234, 1235, 1236, 1237, 2084, 2085–B.

Simancas, Spain. Archivo General de Simancas (AGS).
  Estado, 4628, 8141, 8143, 8151.
  Guerra Moderna (GM), 6091.

Washington, D C. National Archives and Records Service of the United
    States (NARS).
  Domestic Letters of the Department of State (DLDS), M40 r3.
  Miscellaneous Papers of the Continental Congress, 1774–1789 (MPCC),
    M332 r4.
  Papers of the Continental Congress (PCC), M247 r73, 116.
  Records of the Office of Naval Records and Library, Record Group
    (RG) 45, Log-Book of the Frigate South Carolina, 4 August 1781 to
    21 May 1782.
  Revolutionary War Pension and Bounty-Land-Warrant Application
    Files (RWP), M804 r594, 980, 1075, 1661, 2478.

Newspapers

Affiches Américaines (Cape François), 1782.
East Florida Gazette (St. Augustine), 1783.
The London Gazette (London), 1783.
Maryland Journal and Baltimore Advertiser (Baltimore), 1782.
The Pennsylvania Packet (Philadelphia), 1782.
The Royal Gazette (Charleston), 1782.

Books and Journals

"Account of the Large Rebel Frigate, Named the South Carolina, from the
    Laying of Her Keel until Her Capture." The Political Magazine and Par-
    liamentary, Naval, Military, and Literary Journal. London, 1783, 438–40.
Almon, John, ed. The Remembrancer. 2 vols. Picadilly, 1782.
Butterfield, L. H.; and Marc Friedlaender, eds. Adams Family Correspon-
    dence. 4 vols. Cambridge, MA, 1963–73.
Crary, Catherine S., comp. The Price of Loyalty: Tory Writings from the Revolu-
    tionary Era. New York, 1973.
Davenport, Francis Gardiner; and Charles Oscar Paullin. European Treaties
    Bearing on the History of the United States and Its Dependencies. 4 vols. 1917–
    37; rpt. Washington, 1967.

Deane, Silas. *The Deane Papers.* Vol. 22, *Collections of the New York Historical Society.* New York, 1889.

Facts and Observations Justifying the Claims of the Prince of Luxembourg against the State of South Carolina and against Alexander Gillon, Esq., Late Commodore of the Navy of the Said State. [Charlestown, 1784].

Fanning, David. *The Narrative of Col. David Fanning.* Ed. by Lindley S. Butler. Davidson, N C, 1981.

Ferguson, E. James, ed. *The Papers of Robert Morris, 1781–1784.* 7 vols. to date. Pittsburgh, 1973— .

Gillon, Alexander. "Letters from Commodore Gillon in 1778 and 1779." *South Carolina Historical and Genealogical Magazine,* 10(April 1909): 75–82.

"Guia de Forasteros en la Habana ¡Para el Año 1781!" *Memorias de la Sociedad Económica de Amigos del País* (Havana), 15(1845): 109–25.

Historical Manuscripts Commission. *Report on American Manuscripts in the Royal Institutions of Great Britain.* 4 vols. 1904–09. rpt. Boston, 1927.

Miranda, Francisco de. *Archivo del General Miranda.* 24 vols. Caracas, 1929–50.

———. *The New Democracy in America: Travels of Francisco de Miranda in the United States, 1783–1784.* Trans. Judson P. Wood. Ed. John S. Ezell. Norman, OK, 1963.

The Papers of Panton, Leslie, and Company. 26 vols. Microfilm Copy. Woodbridge, CT, 1986.

Pérez Alonso, Manuel Ignacio, S. J., ed. and trans. "War Mission in the Caribbean: The Diary of Don Francisco de Saavedra (1780–1783)." 4 vols. PhD. diss., Georgetown University, 1954.

Rogers, George; and David R. Chesnutt, eds. *The Papers of Henry Laurens.* 10 vols. to date. Columbia, SC, 1968— .

Siebert, Wilbur Henry. *Loyalists in East Florida, 1774 to 1785; The Most Important Documents Pertaining Thereto, Edited with an Accompanying Narrative.* 2 vols. 1929; rpt. Boston, 1972.

Trumbull, John. "Letters of John Trumbull." *Collections of the Massachusetts Historical Society.* 7th ser. 3(1902), 285–89.

SECONDARY SOURCES

Albury, Paul. *The Story of the Bahamas.* New York, 1975.

Bahamas Handbook and Businessman's Annual. Nassau, 1977.

Barney, Mary. *Biographical Memoir of the Late Commodore Joshua Barney.* Boston, 1832.

Barnwell, Stephen B. *The Story of an American Family.* Marquette, WI, 1969.

Beerman, Eric. "José de Solano and the Spanish Navy at the Siege of Pensacola." *Anglo-Spanish Confrontation on the Gulf Coast during the American Revolution,* ed. William S. Coker and Robert R. Rea. Pensacola, 1982. 125–44.

————. "The 1782 American-Spanish Expedition." *Proceedings: United States Naval Institute*. 104(Dec. 1978): 86–87.

Borja Medina Rojas, Francisco de. *José de Ezpeleta: Gobernador de la Mobila, 1780–1781*. Seville, 1980.

Burkholder, Mark A. *Biographical Dictionary of Councilors of the Indies, 1717–1808*. Westport, CT, 1986.

Cashin, Edward J. *The King's Ranger: Thomas Brown and the American Revolution on the Southern Frontier*. Athens, GA, 1989.

Caughey, John Walton. *Bernardo de Gálvez in Louisiana, 1776–1783*. Berkeley, CA, 1934.

Coker, P. C., III. *Charleston's Maritime Heritage, 1670–1865*. Charleston, 1987.

Coker, William S., and Thomas D. Watson. *Indian Traders of the Southeastern Spanish Borderlands: Panton, Leslie and Company and John Forbes and Company, 1783–1847*. Pensacola, 1986.

Coker, William S., and Hazel P. Coker. *The Siege of Pensacola in Maps*. Pensacola, 1981.

Conrotte, Manuel. *La Intervención de España en la Independencia de los Estados Unidos de la América del Norte*. Madrid, 1920.

Craton, Michael. *A History of the Bahamas*. London, 1968.

Edwards, Bryan. *The History, Civil and Commercial, of the British Colonies in the West Indies*. 4 vols. Philadelphia, 1806.

Fairbanks, George R. *History of Florida*. Philadelphia, 1871.

Fisher, Lillian Estelle. *The Last Inca Revolt, 1780–1783*. Norman, OK, 1966.

Forbes, James Grant. *Sketches, Historical and Topographical, of the Floridas; More Particularly of East Florida*. New York, 1821.

Gannon, Michael V. *The Cross in the Sand: The Early Catholic Church in Florida, 1513–1870*. Gainesville, 1967.

Garden, Alexander. *Anecdotes of the American Revolution, Illustrative of the Talents and Virtues of the Heroes and Patriots, Who Acted the Most Conspicuous Parts Therein*. Charleston, 1828.

Grimball, Berkeley. "Commodore Alexander Gillon of South Carolina, 1741–1794." MA thesis, Duke University, 1951.

Holmes, Jack D. L. "Bernardo de Gálvez: Spain's 'Man of the Hour' during the American Revolution." *Cardinales de Dos Independencias (Noreste de México—Sureste de los Estados Unidos)*. Mexico, 1978. 167–74.

Johnson, Joseph. *Traditions and Reminiscences Chiefly of the American Revolution in the South: Including Biographical Sketches, Incidents and Anecdotes Few of Which Have Been Published, Particularly of Residents in the Upper Country*. Charleston, 1851.

Jones, John Paul. *Charges and Proofs Respecting the Conduct of Peter Landais*. New York, 1787.

Kuethe, Allan J. *Cuba, 1753–1815: Crown, Military, and Society*. Knoxville, TN, 1986.

Lambert, Robert Stansbury. *South Carolina Loyalists in the American Revolution*. Columbia, SC, 1987.

Larrabee, Harold A. *Decision at the Chesapeake*. New York, 1964.

———. "A Neglected French Collaborator in the Victory at Yorktown: Claude-Anne Marquis de Saint-Simon (1740–1819)." *Journal de la Société des Américanistes* 24(1932): 245–57.

Lewis, James A. "Anglo-American Entrepreneurs in Havana: The Background and Significance of the Expulsion of 1784–1785." *The North American Role in the Spanish Imperial Economy 1760–1819*, ed. Jacques A. Barbier and Allan J. Kuethe. Manchester, England. 1984. 112–26.

———. "Las Damas de la Havana, El Precursor, and Francisco de Saavedra: A Note on Spanish Participation in the Battle of Yorktown." *The Americas* 37(July 1980): 83–99.

———. "New Spain during the American Revolution, 1779–1783: A Viceroyalty at War." PhD diss., Duke University, 1975.

———. "The Royal Gunpowder Monopoly in New Spain (1766–1783): A Case Study of Management, Technology, and Reform under Charles III." *Ibero-Amerikanisches Archiv* 6(1980): 355–72.

López Canto, Angel. *Don Francisco de Saavedra, Segundo Intendente de Caracas*. Seville, 1973.

McGuffie, T. H. *The Siege of Gibraltar: 1779–1783*. Philadelphia, 1965.

Mackenzie, Roderick. *Strictures on Lt. Col. Tarleton's History "Of the Campaign of 1780 and 1781, in the Southern Provinces of North America": The Recapture of the Island of New Providence*. 1787; rpt. Philadelphia, 1905.

Madariaga, Salvador de. *Bolivar*. Coral Gables, FL, 1952.

Middlebrook, Louis F. *The Frigate South Carolina*. Salem, MA, 1929.

Morison, Samuel Eliot. *John Paul Jones: A Sailor's Biography*. Boston, 1959.

Moss, Bobby Gilmer. *Roster of South Carolina Patriots in the American Revolution*. Baltimore, 1983.

National Genealogical Society. *Index of Revolutionary War Pension Applications in the National Archives*. Washington, 1976.

Oman, Carola. *Nelson*. London, 1947.

Parrish, Lydia Austin. "Records of Some Southern Loyalists: Being a Collection of Manuscripts about Some Eighty Families, Most of Whom Immigrated to the Bahamas during and after the American Revolution." Microfilm Copy. Widener Library, Harvard University, 1940–53.

Parry, J. H. "Eliphalet Fitch: A Yankee Trader in Jamaica during the War of Independence." *History* 40(Feb.–June 1955), 84–98.

Phelan, John Leddy. *The People and the King: The Comunero Revolution in Colombia, 1781*. Madison, WI, 1978.

Porras Muñoz, Guillermo. "El Fracaso de Guarico." *Anuario de Estudios Americanos* 26(1969): 569–609.

Riley, Sandra. *Homeward Bound: A History of the Bahama Islands to 1850 with a Definitive Study of Abaco in the American Loyalist Period*. Miami, 1983.

Robertson, William S. *The Life of Miranda*. 2 vols. Chapel Hill, NC, 1929.

Rodríquez, Mario. *La Revolución Americana de 1776 y el Mundo Hispánico: Ensayos y Documentos*. Madrid, 1976.

Sabine, Lorenzo. *Biographical Sketches of Loyalists of the American Revolution with an Historical Essay*. 2 vols. 1864; rpt. Port Washington, NY, 1966.

Santaló Rodríguez de Viguri, José Luis. *Don José Solano y Bote: Primer Marqués del Socorro, Capitán General de la Armada*. Madrid, 1973.

Schoepf, Johann David. *Travels in the Confederation [1783–84]*. Trans. Alfred J. Morrison. 2 vols. 1911; rpt. New York, 1968.

Smith, D. E. Huger. "Commodore Alexander Gillon and the Frigate *South Carolina*." *South Carolina Historical and Genealogical Magazine* 9(1908): 189–219.

———. "The Luxembourg Claims." *The South Carolina Historical and Genealogical Magazine* 10(1909): 92–115.

———, ed. "The Mission of Col. John Laurens to Europe in 1781." *The South Carolina Historical and Genealogical Magazine* 1(1900): 13–41.

Stone, Richard G. "'The *South Carolina* We've Lost': The Bizarre Saga of Alexander Gillon and His Frigate." *The American Neptune* 29(July 1979): 159–72.

Tebeau, Charlton W. *A History of Florida*. Coral Gables, FL, 1971.

Topping, Aileen Moore. "Alexander Gillon in Havana, 'This Very Friendly Port.'" *The South Carolina Historical Magazine* 83(1982): 34–49.

Tricoche, George Nester. "La Prise de Nassau (Bahamas) par les Loyalistes de la Caroline de Sud en 1783." *Revue des Etudes Historiques* 90(1929): 345–58.

Wright, J. Leitch, Jr. *Florida in the American Revolution*. Gainesville, FL, 1975.

Yela Utrilla, Juan F. *España ante la Independencia de los Estados Unidos*. 2 vols. Lérida, 1925.

INDEX

145